To

....

From

....

Date

....

MORE THAN A
Bucket List

MAKING YOUR DREAMS, PASSION, AND FAITH A REALITY

TONI BIRDSONG

THOMAS NELSON
Since 1798

NASHVILLE   DALLAS   MEXICO CITY   RIO DE JANEIRO

Published in Nashville, Tennessee, by Thomas Nelson.

Thomas Nelson titles may be purchased in bulk for educational, business, fund-raising, or sales promotional use. For information, please e-mail SpecialMarkets@ThomasNelson.com.

Italics in Scripture indicate the author's emphasis.

ISBN-13: 978-1-4003-2079-0 (HC)
ISBN-13: 978-0-529-11286-6 (custom)

Printed in China

14 15 16 17 18 RRD 5 4 3 2 1

www.thomasnelson.com

Contents

Introduction

You'd have a hard time proving this, but most of us agree that the older we get, the faster time seems to speed by. As our time on earth gets shorter, the list of promises we make to ourselves tends to get longer. That's where *More Than a Bucket List* comes in. But this isn't some standard check-it-off bucket list. It's *much* more.

More Than a Bucket List will challenge you to go for that hole-in-one at Pebble Beach, to become an amateur chef, to scale K2. But it will also encourage you to view these accomplishments from God's point of view and to make your bucket list matter *eternally* along the way. With each page, the dream inside you will be drawn out—the higher dream of what God has purposed for you.

So have fun! You can read this book a few different ways. Take in just a few pages a day, or read in blocks and dog-ear what speaks to you as you compile your personal bucket list on the pages provided in the back. For the renegades in the group, close your eyes, crack open the book, and let your finger fall squarely on your next big adventure! Discover hundreds of ideas to jumpstart your heart. Be inspired. Be intentional. And be contagious in your quest to live a life that is more than a bucket list.

Pursue laughter.

Chor•tle *n*: A joyful laugh or chuckle. Word coined by writer Lewis Carroll by combining the words *chuckle* and *snort*.

Laughter reminds us that we are fully alive and that God the Creator is both generous and genius. A buoyant spirit is an invitation to the world to see the joy of heaven God affectionately planted inside you.

If you lack the ability or desire to giggle, belly laugh, twirl with squirrels, or revel in the random, you may be missing out on one of God's most powerful, healing salves for the aches of life.

Convinced that humor is not in your DNA? Ask God to help you get up and over the "What's so funny?" hump. Read—even study—jokes (clean ones), watch comedies, and hang out with clowns (funny friends). Allow yourself to let loose! Before you know it, you'll be unstoppable!

A joyful heart is good medicine, but a crushed spirit dries up the bones.

—Proverbs 17:22 ESV

In fact, let's get started right now! Here are a few points to ponder. Chuckle or groan—it's your call!

- Why don't sheep shrink when it rains?

- Why don't penguins fly? Because they aren't tall enough to be pilots.

- How do they get the deer to cross at that yellow road sign?

- I wondered why baseball was getting bigger. Then it hit me.

- With sufficient thrust, pigs fly just fine.

- Why did the cowboy buy a dachshund? He wanted to get a long little doggie.

Live your dreams.

» Write that book already.

» Attend a red-carpet event. Shine.

» Take your child or grandchild on a special trip, just the two of you. Create a photo album to remember it.

» Learn to play guitar.

» Learn how to surf.

» Protest something publicly (and mind your manners).

» Play the violin—alone, please, if you're an amateur.

» Try every flavor on the Ben & Jerry's menu (not in one sitting!), and refuse to feel guilty.

» Get a good camera, and become a decent photographer.

» Make peace with your in-laws.

» At least once, attend a major sporting event such as the Super Bowl, the Olympics, the Stanley Cup, the World Cup, or the US Open.

Honor the strength of others.

Traveling past a city, you instantly see the brilliance of the skyline stretching up to dominate the sky. The roads and lights pulsate with energy and power. The entire city seems to breathe with possibility. What you don't see is the elaborate matrix of water pipes and power systems that run beneath the streets, pumping, coursing, and supplying the city. If you cut these veins, the city dies. The same is true of the mighty oaks in the park at the center of the city. They tower, sway, and provide refuge and beauty for others. What you don't see is the extraordinary root system that pumps water and nutrients into each trunk.

Many times, the strength of those around us is unseen. It runs deep within them; it finds its wings in the holy places of meditation and prayer and face time with God. Although the world programs us to analyze and assess others instantly, we can't score, evaluate, or even begin to understand the strength that lives in another person. But we must honor it, for it carries life to every soul.

Avoid drawing conclusions based on appearances or stereotypes. Handle others with care, and take time to discover their strengths.

Fight for love.

Throughout history, there have been heroes and warriors of every nation and creed, but no one fought harder for love—and won—than Jesus Christ.

Even when loving rebellious, self-centered, and hateful people shifted from frustrating to deadly, Jesus never quit. He fought, died, and rose again—because of love. But it wasn't just any love. It was a higher love—an absurd, illogical, crazy love not common to this world.

It's that kind of love we're going for. Bring that love to mind when you are tempted to give up on a difficult person, relationship, job, church, or calling.

Pursue love. Make love a habit. Fight to see it rise again.

Be a Good Samaritan.

He was robbed, beaten, and left for dead. A priest passed by. Then a Levite. Both stepped over the river of need that lay quietly heaving at their feet.

Then mercy bent down.

A Samaritan man, moved by pity, stopped to carefully bandage the man's wounds. He then carried him to a nearby inn to recover (see Luke 10).

Step outside youself. Look around. Who are your neighbors? What do they need? Some wounds will be visible, others hidden. At some point, everyone needs a helping hand.

REAL-LIFE CHALLENGE: *Be aware of what's going on around you this week. Cook a meal for that new mom or homebound neighbor. Be the one to help change the flat tire. The next time you see a blood drive, roll up your sleeve.*

Become a more positive person.

It's not a secret. You've been compared to Eeyore on more than one occasion. The invitations have slowed to a trickle, and the crowd splits like the Red Sea when you walk in the room. Maybe you're just going through a negative phase, or maybe your whining, cynicism, and criticism have become a lifestyle that's costing you some serious joy. So how do you become a more positive person? Here are just a few suggestions to get you rolling:

- Admit you've become or are naturally negative.

- Realize you have a choice in how you act.

- Surround yourself with positive people.

- Exercise regularly.

- Laugh out loud. Hey, it works!

- Go serve someone; volunteer.

- Forgive yourself; forgive others.

- Live in the present.

- Practice gratitude.

- Read books about the areas in your life you'd like to improve.

- Get a life coach (or a positive friend) to hold you accountable.

- Do something you love every day.

- Allow God to reshape your heart, thoughts, and words.

Have patience with all things, but chiefly have patience with yourself. Do not lose courage in considering your own imperfections but instantly set about remedying them—every day begin the task anew.

—Francis de Sales

Trust God in business.

Few other situations can sculpt and refine your faith more than trusting God in an entrepreneurial adventure.

An amazingly creative and courageous business life is a roller coaster—risks followed by playing it safe. Great blessing and then being burned. Surviving recessions that take out our neighbors and learning to trust God for each day's manna.

The key to success? Keep moving forward, keep trusting, and refuse dwell on past mistakes. Jesus said in Luke 9:62, "No man, having put his hand to the plough, and looking back, is fit for the kingdom of God" (KJV).

If we are plowing new ground and pursuing the greater adventures God is planting in front of us, looking back only ruins the field for the next harvest. God is concerned about the journey. Trusting Him is the grandest adventure of the Christian's life. That means trusting Him for your business too.

REAL-LIFE CHALLENGE: *Pray over your business daily. Pray for your employees and clients. Ask God for opportunities to serve others and make His name known through the way you do business.*

Tap into the martyr's heart.

Go on! Rack, torture, grind us to powder: our numbers increase in proportion as you mow us down. The blood of Christians is their harvest seed.

—Tertullian

Few of us can truly relate to the possibility of being put to death for our faith. But hundreds of thousands of early Christians met cruelty and hate with courage and heroism. It would be impossible to count those consumed in the fires of persecution that still rage in parts of the world.

Martyrs have been beheaded, crucified, stoned, burned, and dragged through the streets for professing Jesus Christ. Among them are Stephen (the first Christian martyr), Paul, James, Peter, Andrew, and others. Later, the fiery faithful such as Polycarp, William Tyndale, Dietrich Bonhoeffer, and Jim Elliot stepped into heaven as martyrs.

Study the lives of the martyrs as part of your Christian heritage. Their courageous lives laid the groundwork for your ability to worship freely and tell others about Jesus.

Ponder: How did martyrs deal with persecution? What did it cost them daily—and what does it cost you?

REAL-LIFE CHALLENGE: *Help Christians around the world who are being persecuted for spreading the gospel. You can provide medical assistance, food, clothing, and other forms of aid. Go to www.persecution.com to learn more.*

Maintain a balanced digital diet.

Your heart is God's living room. To be specific, it is where the Almighty dwells. So guard that place. Put your life on a balanced digital diet. Limit the stream of information, ideas, ideologies, and opinions daily knocking at the door.

God has allowed you to live in a digital age. That's awesome! Be good at it. But remember: your daily manna and power come from His presence. So recharge daily and fast once in a while.

In quietness and confidence shall be your strength.
—Isaiah 30:15 NKJV

Live with compassion.

» Call your mom and tell her you love her.

» Join a Big Brothers Big Sisters program.

» Become an organ donor.

» Send care packages to people you love.

» Learn CPR.

» Spend time with seniors. Help them record or write their stories.

» Look around. There's always someone more needy than you. Give your time or your resources.

» Adopt a child financially through an established ministry (*www.compassion.com* and *www.worldvision.org* are two great organizations).

» Write each of your kids a letter. Tell them all the things they are doing *right*.

» Affirm with words and deeds the people around you.

» Send birthday cards—via traditional mail.

» Donate blood. Consistently.

Take time to grieve.

Life is hard. No one gets through unscathed. No matter how "good" a life we live, how much money we have, or how many temptations we manage to avoid—suffering is always just a few blocks away. We lose our pets. We lose our friends, and we lose love. We lose jobs, and we lose loved ones. It's okay to take a dive into your suffering. God wired us to cry and grieve. Learn to feel the pain intensely and to really grieve. It's all part of life. God assures us that even our deepest pain will eventually ease (even if that seems unimaginable). Yes, you will hope and laugh again. In John 16:33, Jesus said that in this world, the trouble is gonna come flying at us, "but take heart." We can find peace in His presence and security in the fact that He has overcome the world—and that includes all the suffering.

- Pay attention to your grief. Don't stuff it down deep or sugarcoat it with lines like "God works all things for our good." Job shouted at God. He told God exactly what he was feeling.

- Openly admit your grief to those who are close to you, and ask for their support.

- Try to limit time with people who get in the way of healthy grieving.

- Grieve without distraction.

- Give yourself time, hold on to hope, and connect with grief support resources.

REAL-LIFE CHALLENGE: *Study Isaiah 61, knowing that your pain won't last forever: "to bestow . . . a crown of beauty instead of ashes, the oil of gladness instead of mourning, and a garment of praise instead of a spirit of despair" (v. 3).*

Live a life of love and laughter.

» Learn to juggle. Start with oranges. Move on to bowling pins. As your confidence grows, move on to small children (yes, that was a joke!).

» Make pasta from scratch.

» Become a pogo stick champion.

» Make a list of a hundred books you want to read.

» Stay at a bed-and-breakfast in Vermont.

» Buy twelve-hundred thread count Egyptian cotton sheets—and enjoy hitting the snooze button.

» Sip espresso and write poetry at a Parisian café. Try to look tortured.

» Pick a random talent, and get into the record books.

» Make fire the old-fashioned way.

» Learn at least one cool magic trick for parties.

» Order the sushi you've been afraid to try.

Champion gratitude.

Numerous studies have shown the benefits of gratitude. Some even revealed that people who kept weekly gratitude journals had less aggression, reported fewer physical ailments, and were more optimistic about life compared to people who recorded neutral events and daily hassles.

Gratitude applies a softening salve of peace directly to the callousness caused by life. More than that, giving thanks is applause for the Author of all blessing.

There's really no downside to expressing thanks. Why, then, doesn't it flow more naturally? Perhaps because, like the Israelites, we get spiritual amnesia when life gets tough. Unsanctified expectations of how life *should be* keep us from recognizing and recalling the miracles that hold us upright within this day.

Lifting praise during both trials and blessing distinguishes the Christian. Old Testament prophets like Moses lit up the skies with thanks to God, the psalmist David became a hero of praise, Jesus looked up to heaven and gave thanks, and Paul championed giving thanks "in all circumstances" (1 Thessalonians 5:18).

Gratitude isn't a mental inventory of "blessings" we toss up in the general direction of heaven from time to time. Giving thanks to God is to be a daily, genuine expression of worship that gives glory to God and gives life to us. Gratitude is the glue of relationship.

REAL-LIFE CHALLENGE: *Start a gratitude journal, and make recognizing, recording, and rendering thanks to God (and others) a daily practice.*

Live a life of love and laughter.

» Turn up the music and dance around your kitchen as if no one is watching— and hope no one is!

» Have a food fight.

» Apply to Mensa (manage your expectations).

» Own at least one amazing dog in your lifetime.

» Never let a helium balloon go to waste: announce your candidacy for office, reveal a secret, give an incredible toast, propose.

» Go barefoot in the spring.

» Toss aside the cookbooks, and learn to cook soul food.

» Teach your children or grandchildren how to cook.

» Go shopping in New York City. Wear shades.

» Watch *Anne of Green Gables* with your daughter or granddaughter.

» Celebrate your birthday with a luau. Drink from a coconut.

Rediscover what's important.

Life moves at warp speed. And as desperately as you search for the "halt" lever to stop the train, you just aren't going to find it. It takes intentionality, thought, and commitment to make a true change in your life . . . even as it's speeding by.

If that slow creep of malaise and routine has settled over your heart and mind, stop. Sit down. Take an hour or so and make a list of everything that's important to you. Maybe it's spending more time with family, running a 10K, going back to school, becoming a rock star, or learning how to juggle. Whatever it might be, add *everything* you want to do in life to your list. Now cut that list down to just four or five things. This will be hard to do, but after editing, you will have your core list. This is what matters most. Cut, rearrange, reassemble your life to accomplish the items on your core list today!

REAL-LIFE CHALLENGE: *Make your list, and then do three specific things this week to support the number one thing on your list. Make that call; register for that class; book that plane ticket.*

When it's okay to quit . . .

- Quit judging.
- Quit gossiping.
- Quit cursing.
- Quit flaking.
- Quit condescending.
- Quit being a martyr.
- Quit criticizing.
- Quit wearing masks.
- Quit stretching the truth.
- Quit being selfish.
- Quit being late.
- Quit whining and complaining.
- Quit choosing drama.
- Quit stereotyping.
- Quit being a taker.
- Quit feeling so guilty all the time.
- Quit bringing up the past.
- Quit worrying about the future.
- Quit throwing pity parties.
- Quit pointing at others' sins.
- Quit overindulging.

Trace the steps of Francis of Assisi.

His is a story of *intentionally* going from riches to rags—for the cause of Christ. Born to a life of luxury, Francis of Assisi, through his transformational experiences with God, would become known as "the little poor man of Assisi" and one of the most Christlike men to walk the earth.

Francis lived like a beggar. He wore simple clothes and ate simple food. He loved and befriended God's creatures: the birds and the beasts. He loved the oppressed and the outcast. His life had one channel: communing with God and going from one village to the next talking to people about God's love. He invited people to join him in his humble, God-centered life of service.

The Prayer of Francis of Assisi.

Lord, make me an instrument of peace!
Where there is hatred, let me sow love;
where there is injury, pardon;
where there is error, truth;
where there is doubt, faith;
where there is despair, hope;
where there is darkness, light, and
where there is sorrow, joy.
O Divine Master, grant that I may not
so much seek to be consoled as to console;
to be understood as to understand; to be loved
as to love; for it is in giving that we receive;
it is in pardoning that we are pardoned;
and it is in dying that we are born to Eternal Life.

Live an adventure.

» View the famous northern lights.

» Go parasailing.

» Go deep-sea diving or snorkeling at the Great Barrier Reef.

» Visit the throwback cheese-making village of Grafton, Vermont.

» Go horseback riding on the beach of an exotic island at sunset.

» Go whale watching.

» Visit Cape Cod, Massachusetts's beaches, wetlands, shopping, food, and culture.

» Get lost in Tokyo.

» Eat cannoli in Italy.

» Immerse yourself in another culture.

» Visit Yellowstone National Park. Get your photo taken with Smoky Bear.

» Visit Harrodsburg, Kentucky's Shaker Village of Pleasant Hill, and see the fully restored nineteenth-century buildings where the Quakers once lived.

» Visit Washington state's San Juan Islands. Take a ferry and see the Orca whales.

Forgo the organ recital.

I treasure the memory of my grandmother sitting at her organ and playing "Tiny Bubbles" on Friday nights as *The Lawrence Welk Show* hummed in the background. Unfortunately, that's *not* the kind of organ recital I'm talking about here.

No matter how many physical aches, pains, or procedures you may have as God gifts you with additional years, forgo the urge to share—and bemoan—those details. This kind of organ recital can landlock your mind and your relationships and keep you from your goal of experiencing a full life. Plus, it's kind of annoying.

REAL LIFE CHALLENGE: *When tempted to recite your ailments to others, instead remind yourself of your many blessings, and say, "Tell me what's new and exciting in your life."*

Kiss the sky in Montana.

There's a place on earth that's about five or six miles outside of heaven. It's called Big Sky, Montana. An hour north of Yellowstone National Park, Big Sky has some of the best skiing in the country with more than 3,800 sugary white acres. While you are in Montana, you can also travel to Glacier National Park, called the "Crown of the Continent" for its majestic, rugged peaks. In Montana, it's easy to go from spectacular peaks to incredible valleys (Big Hole Country, Montana) and still not miss a beat when it comes to beauty and awe.

Perfect your elevator speech.

Okay, you only have thirty to sixty seconds to make an incredible, unforgettable, guranteed-to-get-your-foot-in-the-door first impression. What are you going to say? How do you condense a whole career into one minute? Here are some steps: Be concise. Be clear (no jargon). Use powerful words. Tell a story (paint a short visual, e.g., problem→solution). Target your speech (adjust based on who you are talking to). End with a hook (what sets you apart from others?).

REAL-LIFE CHALLENGE: *Practice is the key to a successful elevator speech. Write down and record your elevator speech. Ask a friend to do a few rehearsals with you and offer honest feedback.*

Be a better boss.

- Serve.

- Listen.

- Reward wisely.

- Respond promptly.

- Earn trust.

- Engage directly.

- Show compassion.

- Be consistent.

- Communicate purpose. Often.

- Share opportunity.

Be a true contender.

You'd be hard-pressed to find anywhere in the Bible where God directs believers to argue, quarrel, or squabble with others over the doctrines of the Christian faith. It's easy to fall into the trap of spending more time *defending* our faith to fellow believers than we do *contending* for the faith.

What does it mean to be a contender? It means to know what you believe, know why you believe it, and be able to articulate it humbly, thoughtfully, and biblically to another person. It means expressing your faith in everyday acts of love, service, and faithfulness. Sometimes it means being silent, just as Jesus modeled under fire.

To learn to be a contender, read and apply 1 Peter 3:15, where the apostle said:

> In your hearts set apart Christ as Lord. Always be prepared to give an answer to everyone who asks you to give the reason for the hope that you have. But do this with gentleness and respect.

When we "set apart Christ as Lord," as Peter instructed, we willingly enter into communion with Him. Communion with Jesus is a sanctuary that exists within you—a place to go for fellowship, insight, love, and power that will allow you to step into the world each day as a worthy, mighty contender.

REAL-LIFE CHALLENGE: *Share your faith with another person today without saying a word.*

Go for that dream job.

If you are stuck in a job you don't absolutely love, ask yourself one question: why? What's behind your big fear of doing what you love? Is it financial? Is it physical? Are you afraid of criticism? Are you afraid you aren't good enough? While these fears are real, they likely aren't founded on any kind of truth. That's what fear does—lies and then paralyzes.

You have a limited numbers of hours, days, months, and years to do what God wired you to do. Honor His craftsmanship of you—go, do, be, and excel in your true colors! Here are a few fun facts to inspire you:

- Actor Sylvester Stallone was once a deli counter attendant.

- Famed singer Andrea Bocelli was once a lawyer.

- Chef and author Julia Child was allegedly once a government spy.

- Comedian Rodney Dangerfield was once an aluminum siding salesman.

- Actor Harrison Ford was once a carpenter.

- Bill Gates dropped out of Harvard and failed in his first business before creating the global empire that is Microsoft.

- Light bulb inventor Thomas Edison was an unsuccessful student, was fired from his first two jobs for not being productive enough, and made one thousand unsuccessful attempts before finally creating the design that worked.

- Talk-show queen Oprah Winfrey endured an often abusive childhood as well as numerous career setbacks, including being fired from her job as a television reporter, before becoming one of the richest and most successful women in the world.

- Beloved children's author Theodor Seuss Geisel of *The Cat in the Hat* or *Green Eggs and Ham* was rejected by twenty-seven different publishers for his first book.

Live with strength.

» Don't say yes when you mean no.

» Buy a blender and start making healthy smoothies.

» Spend your time on the real problems, not the imaginary ones.

» Determine to live an outrageously creative life.

» Learn to ask for help when you need it.

» Understand and overcome the fear of death.

» Find a mentor.

» Be a mentor.

» Surrender "that one thing" to God.

» Read the book *Boundaries*. Only keep healthy relationships.

» Right a wrong.

» Don't major in the minors. Let the small stuff go.

Watch less TV.

Everyone has favorite television shows, and everyone needs some downtime. Understood. However, if you consider the stats, you might rethink your viewing habits. According to the A. C. Nielsen Company, Americans spend an average of four hours each day watching television—that's nine years of a sixty-five-year lifespan in front of the tube! It could be time to unplug the TV and replace it with other activities. Play board games, exercise, read, spend time with friends and family, find a hobby, or catch up on your sleep. Just imagine what could be waiting out there beyond the shiny black box!

REAL-LIFE CHALLENGE: *Try to go one week without TV. Keep a journal of the things you did instead. Evaluate the pros and cons of this change. Establish a reasonable viewing schedule.*

Reframe failure.

Have you noticed that there's nothing that God loves more than banged-up believers? There's not a saint in the Old or New Testament that didn't make a mistake or two. Our mistakes are magnets for God to do some of His most brilliant handiwork—if we recognize the holiness of the moment and allow Him to do what He does, which is restore, reconcile, and redeem.

NBA legend Michael Jordan once said, "I've missed more than nine thousand shots in my career. I've lost almost three hundred games. Twenty-six times I've been trusted to take the game-winning shot and missed. I've failed over and over and over again in my life. And that is why I succeed."

REAL-LIFE CHALLENGE: *Reframe a failure as an opportunity for intimacy with God. Then record how God blessed your next steps.*

Aspire to be iridescent.

In the coming-of-age film *Flipped*, based on Wendelin Van Draanen's book, young neighbors Bryce and Juli come to realize that a person's true depth of character is only discovered over time. Eventually, young Bryce says of Juli: "Some of us get dipped in flat, some in satin, some in gloss . . . but every once in a while, you find someone who's iridescent, and when you do, nothing will ever compare."

We all know people dipped in various paints. There are flat (unaffected, one-dimensional spectators), others dipped in satin (smooth-talking, charming, deceitful), and those dipped in gloss (fake, pretentious, vain, predictable).

Iridescence is not so much a color as an effect. An iridescent object has a spectrum of colors that shimmers and changes hue depending on the position from which you view the object. Iridescence is that slight hue of rainbow that can be seen in soap bubbles, seashells, and butterfly wings. The brilliance of something iridescent increases as you begin to appreciate its many shades of beauty.

Through a divine lens, *iridescent* can describe people who are constantly in awe of God. You notice them when they walk into a room. They see God in everything around them. What sets them apart? They've been touched by the unfathomable love of God, and it changed their colors . . . forever. They haven't just *heard* that God is good; they've tasted and seen His goodness up close and personal. They've met with their Father face-to-face, and that encounter has transformed them from flat to iridescent.

REAL-LIFE CHALLENGE: *Watch the movie Flipped. Think about your own iridescence and the iridescence of those around you.*

Live faithfully.

» Serve a day in a charity or ministry that is outside your comfort zone.

» Hold Communion once a month in your home with your family.

» Write out your testimony. Have a long and a short version.

» Go on a mission trip with your child or grandchild.

» Give your testimony in public at least once in your life.

» Don't criticize or complain. Pray.

» Write a love letter to God.

» It's not a suggestion: pray for your enemies.

» Share the gospel with someone who has never heard it.

» Ask someone today, "How can I pray for you?"

» Pray out loud in a group.

» Pray for the guy who just cut you off.

Make peace with persecution.

When Christians are persecuted, they come back stronger because, in their desperation, they come to know and experience God on a deeper level. The greatest Christian revivals in history have followed great periods of persecution. In fact, it has been reported that the Chinese government told officials to pull back on punishing Christians because their numbers were multiplying under oppression. Whether you suffer persecution on a large or small scale, all of it is tough. Jesus warned us about the haters. It's part of the cost of being a disciple of Jesus Christ. And it's worth it.

Facing persecution? Give the enemy two words today: *bring it*.

REAL-LIFE CHALLENGE: *Reframe the attack. Look at it as God's way of testing you and maturing your faith. You will reap blessings and strength!*

Love on your library.

With so many books migrating to the digital world, don't forget your first love: the library. Trek down there today, and reacquaint yourself with books. You know, those pieces of paper cuffed between two awkward cardboard planks. Here are some fun things to do at the library . . . but keep it to a whisper!

- Explore new music.

- Check out a DVD or audiobook.

- Read books from a random section.

- Look through the local author shelf.

- Donate old books.

- Attend a book reading.

- Find out when the next book sale is.

- Be overly kind to and appreciative of librarians. They rock!

Renew your mind each day.

- I am casting down vain imaginations (2 Corinthians 10:5 KJV).

- I am led by the Spirit of God (Romans 8:14 NKJV).

- I am becoming the things I think about (Proverbs 23:7).

- I am exercising my authority over the enemy (Luke 10:19).

- I am being transformed by the renewing of my mind (Romans 12:2).

- I am dressed in garments of praise, not the spirit of depression (Isaiah 61:3).

- I am heir to the blessing of Abraham (Galatians 3:13–14).

- I am being filled with the Spirit (Ephesians 5:18).

- I am clean, set apart, and sanctified (1 Corinthians 6:11).

- I am delivered from the power of darkness (Colossians 1:13 NKJV).

- I am blessed with all spiritual blessings (Ephesians 1:3).

- I am more than a conqueror through Christ (Romans 8:37).

- I am speaking in psalms, hymns, and spiritual songs (Ephesians 5:19).

- I am filling my mind with only good things (Philippians 4:8).

- I am a child of God (Romans 8:16).

- I am redeemed and forgiven of my sins (Ephesians 1:7).

- I am focused on what is unseen and eternal (2 Corinthians 4:18).

- I am shedding the old me
  and putting on the new me
  (Ephesians 4:22–24).

- I am rejoicing always and
  praying without ceasing
  (1 Thessalonians 5:16–17 NKJV).

- I am an overcomer by His blood
  and the word of my testimony
  (Revelation 12:11).

- I am not allowing corrupt
  talk to come from my mouth
  (Ephesians 4:29 ESV).

- I am called with a holy calling
  (2 Timothy 1:9 NKJV).

Get great at everyday romance.

Why settle for good when you can make your relationship great? Some of the longest-wed couples will tell you that they were intentional about keeping the spark in their marriage. Here are just a few ideas for you Romeos or Juliets who've come down with romance amnesia:

- Go on a hayride.

- Book a dinner cruise.

- Eat fish and chips by the sea.

- Renew your vows—as often as you'd like!

- Retire by the ocean.

- Watch old movies together.

- Share a snow cone.

- Meet up each day at 6 p.m. for a kiss.

- Nap in a hammock together.

- Go for a hike; take a gourmet picnic lunch.

- Go to a farm and pick fresh fruit or veggies together. Come home and make something from your harvest.

- Leave kind notes for each other.

- Read Song of Songs to each other.

- Make your sweetheart a mix CD or MP3 playlist of love songs.

- Toast your sweetheart over candlelight.

- Take a dance class.

- Eat ice cream for dinner.

- Carve your initials into a tree.

- Take a cooking class.

REAL-LIFE CHALLENGE: *Pick one of the items above for the beginning of this week, or start planning how you can bring something new to your relationship.*

Live your dreams.

» Star in a talent show.

» Learn to play guitar.

» Take a surfing lesson.

» Hear the Los Angeles Philharmonic play at Frank Gehry's Walt Disney Concert Hall.

» Run a 10K, a half marathon, or the whole 26.2 miles!

» Go without watching television for thirty days.

- » Be a guest instructor in a college class.

- » Learn how to throw a boomerang.

- » Travel solo.

- » Grow your own food.

- » Take an improv comedy class.

- » Bury a time capsule.

- » Right a wrong.

Bless their every step.

I have a quiet, powerful, some might say odd ritual as a mom. Sometimes late at night, as my children sleep, I take a quiet moment to pray . . . over their shoes. I've watched their shoes change over the years from cute little nubs so tiny that they are now Christmas tree ornaments to the tattered sneakers I have to bend over and pick up exactly 546 times a week. But I love their shoes because I love what their shoes represent—the ground they travel, the people they encounter, and the dreams they carry.

In the Bible, feet often represent our walk, heart, or spiritual direction.

- "He set my *feet* on a rock and gave me a firm place to *stand*" (Psalm 40:2).

- "Your word is a lamp to my *feet* and a light for my path" (Psalm 119:105).

- "I have considered my ways and have turned my *steps* to your statutes" (Psalm 119:59).

- "For the Lord will be your confidence and will keep your *foot* from being snared" (Proverbs 3:26).

REAL-LIFE CHALLENGE: *Pray over the shoes of your spouse, your children, or your grandchildren this week. Study the above scriptures. Be conscious of where you place your own feet.*

Sleep in more.

Every once in a while, it really is okay to sleep in. The world is in very good hands. According to the National Sleep Foundation, 40 million Americans don't get enough sleep, which costs nearly $100 billion annually in productivity and medical costs. That makes for one grumpy planet. Chances are, you may be starring in a very cranky life. Lack of sleep contributes to anxiety, car accidents, depression, weight gain, poor decisions, and a compromised immune system. It's just not worth it—so go catch some ZZZZzzzs!

REAL-LIFE CHALLENGE: *Trouble sleeping? Get regular exercise, consume less caffeine, finish eating two to three hours before bed, turn off the TV, and establish a quiet routine (including prayer). Even one hour of extra sleep can make a big difference.*

Make love a verb.

- Love sacrifices.

- Love tells the truth.

- Love bears the big stuff.

- Love believes all things.

- Love endures all things.

- Love lets in.

- Love stands up.

- Love sticks with it.

- Love keeps its cool.

- Love forgives.

- Love accepts.

- Love covers a heap of sins.

- Love crowds out fear.

- Love crushes hate.

Listen and learn from Grandpa.

The older I get, the more I "get" my grandpa and grandma. They were the grandparents who seemed caught in a time warp. You know the ones: they stuck to a schedule, sat quietly on the porch at sunset, rarely purchased anything, and basically . . . did things right by doing things simply and consistently. Here's some Grandpa wisdom for the road:

- Pull over at rest areas.

- Use duct tape—for everything.

- Watch *I Love Lucy*.

- If you're grumpy, take a nap or eat a prune.

- Pick up pennies.

- Wear a wide-brimmed hat in the sun.

- Keep your car oiled.

- Buy American.

- A sandwich is the perfect meal.

- Only brush the teeth you want to keep.

- Buy Rolaids in bulk.

- Tip your hat to strangers.

- Don't complain. Vote.

- Subscribe to *Reader's Digest*.

- Fix what breaks rather than buy a new one.

- Have a favorite chair that's off-limits to everyone else.

- Listen to Johnny Cash.

- Put your faith in God, not in other Christians.

- Bend down when you talk to children.

- Love sincerely.

REAL-LIFE CHALLENGE: *Listen to those who are older this week. Watch what they do, and take notes. They've figured out what works.*

Fall in love with Germany.

Germany has left an indelible mark on my heart. When I was growing up, my family lived there for three years on a military base outside a charming little village named Illesheim. It was magical. The people, the culture, and the beauty of Deutschland captured me and left me aching to return.

I'll never forget the elderly "brotchen lady" who rode her bike to deliver fresh, hot bread to our stairwell every morning at 7 a.m. sharp. Then there was the Spezi (cola and orange soda mix) and beer man who honked his horn in the cul-de-sac every Friday night and the candy lady who flipped open the back of her VW station wagon every Wednesday after dinnertime, revealing a cascade of German chocolates and confections.

Top ten things to do in Germany:

1. Baden-Baden and the Black Forest
2. Castles: Heidelberg, Burg Eltz, and Neuschwanstein
3. Christkindlmarkt during Advent
4. Oktoberfest
5. The architecture of Berlin (and The Wall)
6. The museums of Munich

7. Cathedrals: Aachen and Cologne
8. The Bavarian Alps
9. The 950-year-old city of Nuremburg
10. The concentration camp of Dachau

Also on your must-do list for Germany: drive the autobahn, Germany's expressway system, which does not have a legal speed limit (eighty-one miles per hour is recommended but not required). Ironically, Germany outranks the United States in safety two-to-one.

Live with compassion.

» Skip the chitchat. Go to the heart of the matter. Ask someone, "So, what's God doing in your life lately?"

» At a drive-through, pay the tab of the person in the car behind you.

» Visit Ground Zero.

» Minister in a prison.

» Give a needy child the Christmas of his or her life.

» Visit a concentration camp, and pay your respects.

» Visit Pearl Harbor.

» Start a charity.

» Register to be a bone marrow donor.

» Save a life.

» Help make someone else's dream
come true.

» Adopt a pet.

» Serve on a jury. Give it your all.
Make a difference.

Ask "What if?" for one day.

As an act of grace toward yourself, on this day imagine yourself to be the person you aspire to be. Spend the whole day walking in the blessing and persona of that person. What would you talk about? Where would you go? What kind of attitude would you have? How would you respond to the people around you? In what ways would your life look different?

What if you . . .

Dropped the spirit of criticism? Stopped blaming others? Were less defensive? Held your tongue this time? Jumped to a grace-filled conclusion instead? Had the courage to speak up for the underdog? Were brave enough to have that heart-stopping conversation?

Allow this one day to launch a lifetime of living as the person you aspire to be.

> It is never too late to be what you might have been.
>
> —George Eliot

Live debt-free.

The average American household with a credit card carries more than ten thousand dollars in debt. However, it is possible to live debt-free. People do it every day, and they find that with that discipline comes tremendous freedom. Want some simple ways to get started? Stop using credit; if you have to, cut up your credit cards. Make and stick to a budget. Use the envelope system for cash: divvy up your expenses, and live off only that cash monthly. And when it's gone, it's gone! Learn to live on less. Find ways to make extra income and put that money into a savings account (after you pay off your debt). Establish a rainy-day fund, and make sure you are putting money into a retirement account of some kind.

REAL-LIFE CHALLENGE: *Add up your incoming and your outgoing cash. Establish a budget, and decide how you will stick to it. Do some research on available budgeting tools and methods.*

Accept God's forgiveness.

King David was an adulterer and a murderer. In fact, most Christian leaders today would not be able to maintain their leadership role had they pulled the shenanigans David pulled. Yet David was also called a man after the heart of God (see 1 Samuel 13:14). How could God give the highest expression of love and grace to such a misfit? such a ragamuffin? such an outlaw?

Because God is love—and He is nothing like us. When He loves, He means it. And when He forgives, He means that too.

Still not convinced? Look at these other spiritual misfits God loved like crazy—despite their sin and rough edges.

- Adam and Eve kind of messed it up for all of us.

- Martha (Mary's controlling sis) got a lecture from Jesus at a dinner party. (Can you say, "Awwwwk-warrrrd"?)

- Moses got shut out of the promised land after a forty-year road trip to that very destination.

- Rahab had a *slightly* checkered past, as did the woman at the well.

- The zealous Jew Saul hated and murdered Christians before being reborn as the apostle Paul.

- Matthew was a hated tax collector who was considered a thief.

- Peter followed Jesus for three years— and then denied ever knowing Him.

- The criminal who hung on the cross next to Jesus squeaked into heaven.

REAL-LIFE CHALLENGE: *God's grace extends to anyone who confesses and repents (that means to turn away from your sin). Untangle yourself before God, and give yourself some long-overdue grace.*

Live a life of love and laughter.

» Eat breakfast at Tiffany's in New York. Dress the part.

» Fall in love with old books.

» Make that Hail Mary shot—on the court and in life. (Can you say "Swoosh"?)

» Read poetry aloud with your sweetheart.

» Renew your wedding vows in a fun location—on the beach, in a castle, or on a Ferris wheel!

» Have a mint julep at the Kentucky Derby.

» Go to the Indianapolis 500—and catch the fever!

» Invent something useful. Note: the ShamWow is already taken.

» Rent a karaoke machine, and invite your pals over for some living-room *American Idol*!

» Live with a sense of surprise and expectation.

» Bake your own bread.

» Cross the States by train.

» Make a pie from scratch.

» Eat Peking duck—in Peking.

» Go four wheeling . . . find the mud!

» Visit an Amish community.

» Catch the bouquet—without trampling small children!

» Learn to make sushi.

» Build a birdhouse and enjoy its visitors.

» Befriend a clown. Just don't give him your home address!

Go to the edge.

Come to the edge.

We might fall.

Come to the edge.

It's too high!

COME TO THE EDGE!

And they came,

And he pushed,

And they flew.

—Christopher Logue

Visit Bisbee, Arizona.

Bisbee, Arizona, is a beloved gem of the Southwest. Once a thriving copper-mining town, Bisbee is now home to an eclectic blend of artists, writers, musicians, nature lovers, and retirees. The historic buildings constructed on cascading hill-sides make it hard to believe that at 5,500 feet, this picturesque town sits just fifteen minutes south of the desert icon Tombstone. The locals are friendly and quick to share the legends of gunfights, miners, and ghosts. Since Bisbee is a quietly prestigious hub for live music events and art shows, it's not uncommon to spot a celeb-rity antique shopping along stone streets that seem sealed off from the outside world. A walk-ing tour with local cowboy Michael London and a plunge into the caverns of the earth for the Queen Mine Tour are each a must.

Seek out the bizarre.

The following conventions really do exist. If you are looking for something out of the ordinary, you don't have to look very far. Have fun at the:

- Bald Is Beautiful Convention in Morehead City, North Carolina

- Summer Redneck Games in East Dublin, Georgia

- World Toe Wrestling Championship in Ashbourne, England

- Zombie Walk at Monroeville Mall outside Pittsburg, Pennsylvania

- World's Biggest Liar Competition in Wasdale, England

- Typewriter Toss in Springfield, Missouri

- Stiletto Run in Berlin, Germany

- Bonnie and Clyde Festival in Gibsland, Louisiana

- Great Whipped Cream Battle in the Czech Republic

- Pancake Day Races in London, England

- Cockroach Races in Brisbane, Australia

- Monkey Buffet Festival in Lopburi, Thailand

- Tuna Tossing Festival in Australia

- Roswell UFO Festival in Roswell, New Mexico

- Maslenitsa Fist Fighting in Russia

- Cheese-Rolling Festival in Gloucestershire, England

- Food Fight Festival (*La Tomatina*) in Buñol, Spain

- 24-Hour Marriage Marathon in New York, New York

- Calaveras County Fair and Jumping Frog Jubilee in Angels Camp, California

- Burger Fest in Seymour, Wisconsin

- O. Henry Pun-Off in Austin, Texas

- Dukes of Hazzard Fan Club Convention in Covington, Georgia

Experience the real Ireland.

"There are only two kinds of people in the world," or so the saying goes: "the Irish and those who wish they were." If you've been to Ireland, you're nodding your head and understand the country's heartbeat beyond the images of shamrocks, shillelaghs, and leprechauns.

Rolling emerald countrysides and breathtaking cliffs have likely branded Ireland's beauty onto your heart. But there's nothing quite like stepping into this God-painted gem and experiencing it firsthand. The people, music, and culture are destinations in themselves. Who doesn't love a night of folk music, dancing, and shouting limericks? Or visiting the birthplace of icons like U2, the Undertones, the Chieftains, Yeats, and Joyce? Ireland is also considered one of the leading golf destinations, has reputable surfing, and boasts the world's leading horticulture. Must-sees: Connemara, Aran Islands, Bru na Boinne, Derry, Glengesh Pass, Clonmacnoise, Kilkenny, Beara Peninsula, West Belfast, and Skellig Michael, an incredible sixth-century island monastery. Walking Killarney National Park's lakes and misty mountains and the Cliffs of Moher in Clare County will return you home forever changed.

A little-known fact: the shamrock actually became widely known when Saint Patrick preached the doctrine of the Trinity and used the shamrock as a symbol of its great mystery. Today, the shamrock is worn in Ireland and America to celebrate Irish heritage. Shamrock plants are grown in County Cork, Ireland, and shipped all over the world for Saint Patrick's Day.

Live an adventure.

» Go on a camel trek in Egypt.

» Eat crepes in France.

» Take a Zumba class.

» Visit Washington, DC. See every single thing.

» Eat authentic local cuisine from street carts in Bangkok, Thailand.

» Visit Mount Rushmore. (No, Virginia, it's not a natural wonder.)

» Ride a steamboat down the Mississippi River.

» Participate in a Japanese tea ceremony.

» Ride an elephant (avoid rush hours in big cities).

» Visit Buckingham Palace. Wear a tiara.

» See the architectural wonders of Columbus, Indiana

» Visit Cannery Row in Monterey, California.

» Attend a gunfight at noon in the streets of Tombstone, Arizona. Then go to the O.K. Corral and drink an ice-cold sarsaparilla.

Run *your* race.

A prize racehorse trains with blinders on. Blinders allow the horse to stay focused and not to be spooked by distractions or by the maneuvers of the other horses and jockeys.

When the apostle Paul encouraged Timothy (and us) to run the race set before us and to keep our eyes on the prize, he was urging us to stay focused by saying, "You aren't the first; you won't be the last. You can do this . . . and heaven is gonna be worth it!"

> Since we are surrounded by such a great cloud of witnesses, let us throw off everything that hinders and the sin that so easily entangles, and let us run with perseverance the race marked out for us.
>
> —Hebrews 12:1

REAL-LIFE CHALLENGE: *What are the things, people, or fears distracting you today? Write them down, and work on a game plan to overcome them. Like a racehorse, condition your life daily for the race. Ask God to help.*

Go beyond the 'burbs.

Just thirty minutes to the north, south, east, or west of your home, there's likely a poor neighborhood or town that the world has all but forgotten. You don't have to travel the globe to find hunger, disease, poverty, and people whose hope is tapped out. So take a drive. Look at these forgotten neighbors; look at the people's faces, where they live, and what kind of resources they have. Consider what you can do to help.

REAL-LIFE CHALLENGE: *Call the homeless shelter, community center, or a church in one of these neighborhoods. Find out how you can assist. Think about giving your time, expertise, and money to help these neighbors.*

Don't wonder any longer . . .

- what your childhood friend is doing now.

- what life would be like if you forgave that one person.

- what you would try if you weren't afraid of failing.

- what would happen if they really knew how you felt.

- what you could have been.

- what true love feels like.

- what you'd look like as a size 6.

- what it feels like to conquer that one big fear.

- what would happen if you asked for forgiveness.

- what it's like to finish a marathon.

- what life would be like if you lived with greater faith.

- if your kids could understand how much you love them.

- what it feels like to be healthy.

- if your parents realize how grateful you are for them.

- what it feels like to get up on stage and perform.

- what it's like to worship with abandon.

- if you should write that book.

- what life would be like if you really could let go.

REAL-LIFE CHALLENGE: *This week, do two activities on the list above. Do two more next week, and the week after that, and so on. Pretend you just got the lead role in . . . your life!*

Live with strength.

» Find your unique superpower, and don't be afraid to use it. Can you see through people? leap over any life obstacle? Are you a peacemaker? a motivator?

» Go on a creative retreat.

» Expect the best from people

» Stick up for the underdog.

» Do what you can to change *you*.
  Leave other people to God.

» Stop being afraid.

» Believe in—and expect—miracles.

» Be teachable.

» Know what you stand for and why.

» Push your fitness level up a notch.

» Become a recovering perfectionist.

» Live debt-free.

» Study integrity and humility. Aspire to a life committed to both.

» Look for and wave to angels.

Try every bonbon on the planet.

You read that correctly. You now have permission to go on a bonbon-tasting spree. A great place to start is Belgium, where some of the world's finest chocolate is made—and consumed!

Annually, worldwide consumption of chocolate averages approximately six hundred thousand tons, and Belgian chocolatiers joyfully feed that frenzy. It's said that Belgians have a passion for chocolate equal to that of the Aztecs, who considered the cocoa bean a god. But be warned: Belgium is a place where you could easily slip into a chocolate coma as you discover the joys inside each bonbon: there's cognac butter cream, orange- and coffee-flavored crème fraîche, chocolate ganache, liqueurs, and many other hidden delights. Belgian bonbon shops to visit: Le Chocolatier Manon, Neuhaus, Wittamer, Chez Nihoul, and Godiva.

Honor your season.

What seems permanent is temporary. God's kind, wise, sovereign hand has put in motion a life cycle that is *perfectly* synchronized with heaven. When you have lost your true north and can't feel the light on your face, read Ecclesiastes, and find comfort in your season. God is there with you.

> *There is a time for everything, and a*
> *season for every activity under heaven:*
> *a time to be born and a time to die,*
> *a time to plant and a time to uproot,*
> *a time to kill and a time to heal,*
> *a time to tear down and a time to build,*
> *a time to weep and a time to laugh,*
> *a time to mourn and a time to dance,*
> *a time to scatter stones and a time to*
> *gather them,*
> *a time to embrace and a time to refrain,*
> *a time to search and a time to give up,*
> *a time to keep and a time to throw away,*
> *a time to tear and a time to mend,*
> *a time to be silent and a time to speak,*
> *a time to love and a time to hate,*
> *a time for war and a time for peace.*
>
> —Ecclesiastes 3:1–8

Keep church simple.

It's a hard lesson to learn *Hmmm. Was that God calling me to lead that ministry, or was I just trying to impress the pastor*? It's so easy to complicate things God intended to be simple. We overdo. We overcommit. Then we overreact when we get burned out. It's an unofficial Christian ritual that is taking place in churches everywhere.

Henry Blackaby, in his book *Experiencing God*, encourages believers to always be asking the question, "Where is God at work?" Asking that question can be extremely helpful in determining where to serve.

God isn't wringing His hands trying to figure out who will build His church or what name tags and titles to pass out. He's whispering to you quietly, hoping you will turn to Him faithfully so He can bless you with a front-row seat to what He's doing right now, in your midst. Corrie ten Boom said it best: "Trying to do the Lord's work in your own strength is the most confusing, exhausting, and tedious of all work. But when you are filled with the Holy Spirit, then the ministry of Jesus just flows out of you."

REAL-LIFE CHALLENGE: *Take a breath before you say yes. Look to discover where God may be at work so that you can join Him.*

Live faithfully.

» Memorize one Bible verse a week.

» Read 1 Corinthians 13. Replace every occurrence of the word *love* with your name.

» Listen. Better than that.

» Respond to a big offense or hurt by showing even bigger love.

» Celebrate more—the small things as well as the big things.

» Hush. Go on a word fast.

» Give those around you more grace.

» Fight for love. Don't give up.

» Forgive your spouse.

» Watch *The Jesus Film* at least once.

Live 100 percent complaint-free.

Live complaint-free for thirty days. Try it. You may like it—and chances are the people around you will be absolutely giddy about it. When you catch yourself scoring the waitress's performance or rolling your eyes at the crying baby in church—check your heart. Ask God to flood you in that moment with His love and His grace.

As God's chosen people, holy and dearly loved, clothe yourselves with compassion, kindness, humility, gentleness and patience.
—Colossians 3:12

Find your passion.

- What activity makes you lose track of time?

- What connects your soul to God?

- What would you do even without pay?

- What sparks your creativity?

- What puts a smile on your face?

- What would you regret not having tried?

Love your community.

Pick up the local paper.
Ask yourself:

▶ Who are my neighbors?

▶ How can I help for them?

- How can I pray for them?

- Why has God put me in this specific place?

- Where can I volunteer?

- Who in my everyday world might I encourage or thank?

- What injustice can I work toward stopping?

Don't zoom past the riches.

How many riches have we rushed past on our way to fill our hours? Slow down. Relax. Take time to consider how much God loves you and how far His love will go to find you. Here's His message (creatively paraphrased) for you today and always:

- You are My beloved child (Ephesians 5:1).

- I knew you before you were born. As My hands formed you, I whispered purpose into your bones. I can't *not* love you (Psalm 139:1–6).

- My love is contrary to all you know of love. I love you "even though" and "deeper still." My love reaches, pursues, remains (Psalm 36:5).

- My love for you won't walk out, fail, or ever come to an end (Deuteronomy 31:8).

- No matter what you've heard or what you've come to believe, nothing can separate you from My love (Romans 8:38–39).

- I am not like people. So please don't put human words in My mouth or apply human behaviors to My character. You will miss Me altogether (Isaiah 55:8).

- I understand your pain and heartbreak. And My heart breaks with yours (Isaiah 53:3).

- There's nowhere you can go where My love won't find you (Psalm 139:7–8).

- The shame and guilt that weigh you down have been taken care of on the cross. Your account has been zeroed out (John 3:16).

- The addictions. The pride. The selfishness. The hate. The lust. The jealousy. The critical spirit. The greed. I can heal it. All of it. You can start fresh. Today (Romans 8:1–4).

Live your dreams.

» Slow dance with your sweetheart in the falling snow.

» Simplify. Give away all that stuff.

» Take a painting class.

» Go to a symphony. Close your eyes. Pick out the many layers of sound. Enjoy every moment. Thoroughly.

» Make at least one awesome scrapbook of your life. Pass it down.

» Treat fun and pleasure as necessities, not luxuries.

» Kiss your sweetheart under a waterfall in Hawaii.

» Become an amazing storyteller.

» Learn how to catch, clean, and cook a fish.

» Fly first-class just once. And enjoy that cheese platter!

» Stand under a redwood tree and look up.

» Learn sign language.

Celebrate more.

How many times do you let a birthday, anniversary, or special accomplishment simply slip away with little revelry? Go overboard for a friend's birthday. Commemorate your anniversary with real fireworks. Surprise your staff with a "small wins" celebration: take time to call out ten successes over the past month. Take your friend to lunch to celebrate a promotion or an answered prayer. When we celebrate the big and the little things, we live out God's blessings in 3-D and honor the joys taking place all around us.

REAL-LIFE CHALLENGE: *This month, choose one big and one little thing to celebrate—and be creative!*

Focus on the promises, not the problem.

- God has a plan for you, and it's awesome. You just can't see it right now (Jeremiah 29:11).

- God will take this problem . . . if you let Him (Matthew 11:28–29).

- He'll give you new strength for this crisis. You're gonna soar (Isaiah 40:29–31).

- He will supply all your needs. Relax (Philippians 4:19).

- No matter what things look like, they're going to be okay (Romans 8:37–39).

- God's given you the gift of peace. Have you opened it? (John 14:27).

- You have the free gift of eternal life. That makes everything on earth doable (Romans 6:23).

Live within your harvest.

Money can be so difficult to hold on to. Don't let a lack of funds keep you from living your dreams. Just a few things to keep in mind about holding on to your cash:

- Don't fall for advertising gimmicks.

- Don't shop when you are sad, tired, or hungry.

- Take time to create a budget. Then stick to it.

- Don't try to keep up with the Joneses—they don't exist.

- Buy used books instead of new.

- Skip name brands—but don't scrimp on quality.

- Shop the perimeter of the grocery store, where the fresh, unprocessed food is.

- Don't buy on credit.

- Keep your car as long as you can.

- Brown-bag your lunch.

- Buy a car that's good on gas.

- Carry cash. Don't get addicted to using your debit or credit card.

Don't spend your life online.

Life is short and time is precious. If you are going to surf, let it be on a board off the Gulf Coast after a spring storm—not aimlessly on the Internet. As Christians, we can't make a difference in this world unless we *are* different. So be a good steward of your time online; have a purpose and a plan. Here are five questions, taken from *stickyJesus.com*, that will help you keep your focus when you're online.

1. *What's my plan and purpose for being online?* Are you chatting without a point? Stop. Pray. Ask the Holy Spirit to lead you in a plan for your online time.
2. *Am I majoring in the minors?* Do you complain, judge, make sarcastic comments, post random nothings, or criticize others? Use your online time to share hope and lift others.
3. *What would Jesus tweet?* Please—be interesting, funny, creative, unique, and opinionated. Just don't allow bold, unique "you" to clash with the holiness and majesty of Christ.

4. *Am I influencing culture, or is culture influencing me?* Are you fixed in your purpose and standing your ground, or are you easily swayed by the cultural banter, music, news, and assortment of morals swirling around you?

5. *Does my digital footprint point others toward heaven?* If you added up your posts, comments, photos, profiles, tweets, and "likes," would they point others toward heaven or confuse them about who Jesus is and why He came?

REAL-LIFE CHALLENGE: *Place your Bible on your laptop before you go to bed each night—kind of like a padlock. This will remind you to pray before you get online each day.*

Feeling extreme? What are you waiting for?

» Dive the cenotes of the Yucatán.

» Bike the Baja Peninsula.

» Summit Everest (or hike to base camp).

» Surf the North Shore on Oahu, Hawaii.

» Hike the Triple Crown: the Appalachian Trail, the Pacific Coast Trail, and the Continental Divide Trail.

» Climb Java's volcanoes.

» Free climb Yosemite's El Capitan.

» Climb, swim, or surf the Poles—as in the Arctic and Antarctic.

» Climb the Seven Summits, the seven highest mountains on the seven continents.

» Dive the Blue Holes in the Bahamas.

» Ski Denali, North America's tallest mountain.

» Take a camel trek in Morocco.

» Kayak or raft the Zambezi.

» Trek the Mont Blanc Circuit.

» Raft the Grand Canyon.

Live with compassion.

» Help a young person jump-start his or her career.

» Pick up the check at a restaurant for a police officer, firefighter, or member of the military.

» Salute a soldier. Tell him or her thank you.

» Surprise a friend with a gift—and don't identify the giver!

» Volunteer at an animal shelter.

» Pay for a single mom's groceries.

» Set aside one afternoon a month to write thank-you notes and love letters. Mail them.

» Grow your hair out, and then donate it to Locks of Love.

» Take a homeless person to lunch. Listen to his or her story.

» Become skilled at giving.

» Become skilled at receiving.

» Be part of a relief effort.

» Adopt a soldier during his or her tour of duty.

Zip it and listen.

For a full day, don't talk. Just listen. Listen to the people around you. What are they saying? What are they not saying? What are their needs? When there's a pause, respond with, "Tell me more." Refrain from offering advice, interrupting, turning the conversation back to yourself, or adding anything outside of what they are expressing to you.

Track down "that" teacher.

That special individual raised your chin, looked you straight in the eye, and said, "I believe in you." Track down that teacher or mentor who flipped your confidence switch. Maybe it's a scout leader, an uncle or aunt, or a Sunday school leader. Write a letter and tell that person how knowing him or her impacted you. If you are close by, pay a visit or take him or her out for a thank-you dinner.

Memorize the
Serenity Prayer
(at least the first part).

God, grant me the serenity to accept the things I cannot change, courage to change the things I can, and wisdom to know the difference.

Living one day at a time; enjoying one moment at a time; accepting hardship as the pathway to peace. Taking, as He did, this sinful world as it is, not as I would have it; trusting that He will make all things right if I surrender to His will; that I may be reasonably happy in this life and supremely happy with Him forever in the next. Amen.

—Reinhold Niebuhr

Preach heaven's message first.

It may come as a shock to some believers to discover that Jesus wasn't a registered Republican or Democrat. He wasn't patriotic; He didn't crusade for baby seals, picket against poverty, or pin a colored ribbon on His chest.

It isn't that He didn't care about these things—we know He did because He created all things. He just cared about heaven *more*. Since redemption of sin is the only way to get there, redemption of sin is what Jesus preached first. He came to rehabilitate and ready us for heaven. His allegiance, His crusade, and His colors were tethered to His hometown. If anyone looking on doubted that, the cross soon clarified Jesus' primary affiliations.

Does following Jesus mean you abandon all other passions and platforms? Absolutely not. Just abide in Him—first. Lift His message—highest. Let the message of the cross be what you stand up for and the only message you bow down to. Exchange your prejudices and points of view for His. There's a lot of chatter in the world. But when you follow Christ, you are marked by and for the message of the gospel.

Like Jesus, let Calvary be the flag you lift highest, the passion that prevails. All other flags—even the "good stuff" like grace, goodness, service, our politics, and our principles—all are far less important than the cross. Hopefully, we will, like the apostle Paul, someday say: *For I am compelled to preach. Woe to me if I do not preach the gospel!*

God's truth will always bring out the toxins of this world. No one knew this better than Jesus—a magnet for persecution but a master at maintaining His cool. Thankfully, He taught us how to respond when the bullets fly and that incredible things can happen when we *choose* His ways over our own.

REAL-LIFE CHALLENGE: *Evaluate your emotional and spiritual ranking system. What passions and messages come first in your life?*

Live a life of love and laughter.

» Play the ukulele on the beach or while sitting in a tree.

» Make gifts instead of buying them.

» Learn to play Scrabble. Well.

» Send out handmade Valentine's Day cards in the mail.

» Revive the tradition of making a toast at social gatherings.

» Send someone a message in skywriting.

» Visit the birthplace of Superman: Metropolis, Illinois.

» Throw more dinner parties.

» Break the sound barrier. With your laugh.

» Lie in a hammock and watch the little white seed puffs float by.

» Buy something from an infomercial.

» Befriend people who are different. Step out of your comfort zone.

» Learn the basics of social networking.

» Audition for a game show.

» Make homemade jam.

Praise others— because you can.

Praise is powerful—especially when it's directed at others. Make an effort to praise or encourage the people around you. Tell your kids or grand-kids what they are doing right. Compliment your spouse. Tell your employees you appreciate them. Give the cashier a sincere "thank you." Praise can lift the moment, the day, or someone's spirits.

The most important thing to remember is to keep praise real. Authentic praise sticks to a person's heart, but disingenuous, fluffy praise is unhelpful and can even be hurtful (and can really unsettle people).

Ignore your critics.

It is not the critic who counts: not the man who points out how the strong man stumbles or where the doer of deeds could have done better. The credit belongs to the man who is actually in the arena, whose face is marred by dust and sweat and blood, who strives valiantly, who errs and comes up short again and again, because there is no effort without error or shortcoming, but who does actually strive to do the deed; who knows the great enthusiasms, the great devotions, who spends himself for a worthy cause; who, at the best, knows, in the end, the triumph of high achievement, and who, at the worst, if he fails, at least he fails while daring greatly, so that his place shall never be with those cold and timid souls who knew neither victory nor defeat.

—Teddy Roosevelt

Bicycle through Provence.

Enjoy the captivating countryside of Provence, France—on your bike. Pedal alongside fields of colorful blooms and through quaint hilltop villages, and stop along the way for incredible food. Begin in L'Isle-sur-la-Sorgue, the "Little Venice" of Provence; then head toward the foothills of Mont Ventoux. You'll see some of the most picturesque villages in Provence, including Venasque and Crillon le Brave. Continue your voyage to the medieval beauty of Vaison la Romaine, and see its Roman ruins. Enjoy the slower pace of cycling your way through all these breathtaking locales, wind at your back and the sights, smells, and sounds of Provence directly beneath your two wheels.

Remember the miracles.

The waters were high. The Jordan River was now the only barrier to the promised land. It felt as if forty years of wandering had welled up at the river's edge. It was impassable.

But then God . . .

To honor their covenant with God, the Israelites set up standing stones as a reminder of God's supernatural act in parting the Jordan that day (Joshua 4).

Remembering the miracles, big and small, that God has orchestrated throughout our lives is the secret to living a big life. Join the ranks of Joshua, Jacob, Moses, and Peter.

"In the future when your descendants ask their fathers, 'What do these stones mean?' tell them, 'Israel crossed the Jordan on dry ground.'"

—Joshua 4:21–22

REAL-LIFE CHALLENGE: *Set up stones in your home or business. Write on them. Record the significant movements of God in your life: the rescues, the miracles, the wonders, your awe.*

Invite wisdom to dinner.

Observing God's faithfulness up close and personal trumps any book you could read or any seminary class you could take.

So the next time you have friend over, do something life influencing. Invite as your guest of honor a wise, older, faithful believer. And just listen.

Ask that person candid questions about his or her faith, such as:

- At what specific moments did God show up in your life?

- What do you do to you keep your faith fresh and growing?

- How did you make it through your worst storm?

- When and how do you hear from God?

- What can I do personally to persevere?

{ **The lips of the wise spread knowledge.**
—**Proverbs 15:7** }

Live an adventure.

» Go on a Disney cruise.

» Visit a planetarium.

» (Watch other people) run with the bulls in Pamplona.

» Visit the Fontana di Trevi, the most beautiful fountain in Rome. Make a wish.

» Ride in a blimp.

» Take the waters at a hot spring.

- » Experience the Twelve Apostles, a famed series of limestone stacks off the shore of Australia.

- » Visit Mesa Verde National Park in Colorado, and see ruins of villages built by the Pueblo people in the 1200s.

- » Drive a NASCAR track.

- » Visit a volcano. Don't talk above a whisper.

- » Stay in an ice hotel.

- » Ride a motorcycle south on US 1 in California.

Master a short course in human relations.

The **six** most important words: I admit that I was wrong.

The **five** most important words: You did a great job.

The **four** most important words: What do you think?

The **three** most important words: Could you please . . .

The **two** most important words: Thank you.

The **most** important word: We.

The **least** important word: I.

—anonymous

Reduce your carbon footprint.

You can't see it, but the earth can feel it—the weight of your personal carbon footprint. A carbon footprint is the amount of greenhouse gases (including carbon dioxide) caused by a person, family, event, industry, and so on. Practice the three Rs: reduce, reuse, and recycle. Recycle plastics, glass, paper, and cans. Donate old clothing, and try riding your bike reasonable distances instead of driving. A few other tips: take direct flights, use cold water instead of hot, unplug appliances when they are off, buy products with minimal packaging, and ditch bottled water. Every little bit counts.

REAL-LIFE CHALLENGE: *If you don't already recycle, read up on it and outfit your home to make recycling easy. Call your city and get the facts.*

Bust out of your rut.

One sure way to miss out on the beauty around you is to get so into your routine that you end up in a rut. There's a lot to be said for order—until that order chokes out your vision and creativity. Change things up. Inject spontaneity into your week. Surprise yourself by trying new food, listening to new music, reading books, meeting new people, and visiting a new museum or city. Go a step further and examine the mental ruts you've fallen into that keep you from pursuing bigger goals or even a bigger faith.

James 1 teaches us how important it is to have patience when we're changing and growing. Don't be surprised if, when you start to break familiar patterns, you run into opposition. We need to be patient with ourselves when we're trying to make changes.

> Perseverance must finish its work so that you may be mature and complete, not lacking anything.
> —James 1:4

REAL-LIFE CHALLENGE: *Shake things up a bit by taking a new route to work or trying a new restaurant. Get out a map, and take a one-day trip to someplace completely new! Small risks can bust ruts and lead us to hunger for bigger things and healthy changes.*

Go on a word fast.
Record what you hear.

We bemoan that we can't hear from God, that we are confused and frustrated about what to do, which way to go, and that God just isn't . . . well . . . moving fast enough.

Have you considered giving your lips the day off? Go on a word fast for half a day or a full day. You might be amazed at the clarity of His voice and the power that emerges when you stop talking and actually listen to God.

The heavens declare the glory of God;
the skies proclaim the work of his hands.
Day after day they pour forth speech;
night after night they reveal knowledge.
There is no speech or language
where their voice is not heard.
Their voice goes out into all the earth,
their words to the ends of the world.
—Psalm 19:1–4

Some of the Pharisees in the crowd said to Jesus, "Teacher, rebuke your disciples!" "I tell you," he replied, "if they keep quiet, the stones will cry out."

—Luke 19:39–40

Wash the feet of another.

Peter's heart was beating wildly. He could see Jesus coming closer. *Please don't*, he thought. *How can the Messiah stoop so low?* John 13 records the act of Jesus washing the disciples' feet, one of the most powerful acts of love and humility of His ministry.

Once Peter understood the holiness of the moment, he offered Jesus not only his feet but also his hands and head for washing.

The act of washing someone else's feet can be life changing for you and for the other person. This single, sacred gesture personifies the heart of Christ and can communicate forgiveness, unconditional love, heavenly unity, and new life.

REAL-LIFE CHALLENGE: *Summon the courage and humility to wash the feet of someone in your life. Do you need a fresh start with that person? Does that person need to understand God's love and forgiveness? Often this intimate act wisely and prayerfully.*

Earn the right to wear red.

My mother wears red. A lot. It's striking against her black hair and big brown eyes. But that's not why she wears red. She wears red because she has earned it. She has earned the brief glances and silent applause she receives when she walks in a room that says, "Bravo. Bravo for you, beautiful one." She has fought the good fight and emerged with grace. She has tangoed with tears and led the dance.

She wears red because comebacks are beautiful, and only red will do.

Live with strength.

» Go ahead and cry. Great love brings true tears—of both joy and sadness.

» Follow through. Don't leave people hanging.

» Return a favor.

» Paint a room the color you *really* want to paint it.

» Never show up empty-handed.

» Sharpen your wit.

» Be incurably brave.

» Get rid of the stuff (including people) that zap your spiritual pursuits, creativity, and energy.

» State your age without a hint of regret.

» Become an expert at conflict resolution.

» Never give up.

» Lose ten pounds in one hour— give God your troubles.

Live. Greater.

The great painter and sculptor Michelangelo came into the studio of Raphael and looked at one of Raphael's early drawings. Hastily, he took a piece of chalk and wrote across the drawing *Amplius*, which means "greater" or "larger." Michelangelo immediately saw Raphael's plan as too small. His artist's eye saw greatness and depth where Raphael had held back.

If God were to walk into your life today and reach for the chalk, would your heart beat with anticipation at what He might write, or with fear that he might write *amplius* across your life?

What will you do about that anticipation or fear?

Be okay with a nothing day.

▶ Stay in your pj's.

▶ Watch movies. Lots of 'em.

▶ Revel in the intense artistry of bed head.

▶ Leave the dishes in the sink. Ignore their screams.

▶ Bond with your pet.

▶ Admire the slimming effect fuzzy socks have on your legs.

▶ Every time you pass a mirror, say something nice to yourself and wave at the reflection.

Visit the Holy Land.

Stepping onto the ground where Jesus, David, Peter, and Paul walked can change one's life. For some, a visit to the Holy Land is just another tour, but for most it's a sacred immersion in the spaces, towns, hillsides, and rivers where God wove our spiritual heritage.

In Nazareth you can see the Basilica of the Annunciation built over the place where the angel Gabriel told Mary she would be the mother of the Savior and where Jesus' family once lived. You can visit Bethlehem where Jesus was born, Galilee, where He preached the Sermon on the Mount, the Garden of Gethsemane, where He cried out to God, and the Church of the Holy Sepulchre, built on the site where Jesus was crucified. You can walk the streets the six-thousand-year-old city Jaffa, where Jonah set sail for Nineveh and where Peter began his ministry.

Imagine the pure adventure and resulting awe that come with visiting the tomb of King David and the room of the Last Supper and seeing the scriptures come to life in Jericho, the Jordan Valley, Tiberius, the Sea of Galilee,

Capernaum, and many, many other holy sites. If you decide to travel to this region of the Middle East, be ready for a tsunami of emotion. It's a journey that bears evidence of the many chapters of God's plan to redeem humankind. Be prepared to step into a land spilling over with history, hope, bloodshed, and blessing.

REAL-LIFE CHALLENGE: *Open a special savings account for a pilgrimage to the Holy Land.*

Refresh yourself on the Big Ten.

Are you like most people? Do you "kinda know" the Ten Commandments? Do you go around telling people not to commit the act of eating poultry or cover up their neighbor's stuff? Maybe it's time to plant God's commands a little deeper . . . just to be safe.

1. You shall have no other gods before me.
2. You shall not make for yourself any graven image.
3. Remember the Sabbath day, to keep it holy.
4. You shall not take the name of the Lord your God in vain.
5. Honor your father and your mother.
6. You shall not kill.
7. You shall not commit adultery.
8. You shall not steal.
9. You shall not bear false witness against your neighbor.
10. You shall not covet your neighbor's wife or possessions.

—based on Exodus 20:1–17

Refuse to grow up— completely.

When Jesus said, "Let the little children come to me," He was talking to adults as well as kids. He was telling us to mimic the kids: to fling our hearts open wide and obliterate the boxes we've put God in. To embrace faith with wild abandon, be teachable, and trust God as a child would trust a parent. Sounds easy enough, right?

What can we learn from kids? To express our ideas boldly, to dream ginormous dreams, to live fully in the moment, to taste crazy foods, to take risks, to be wildly creative and contagiously optimistic, and to trust God wholeheartedly.

REAL-LIFE CHALLENGE: *The next time you are around a child or a group of younger people, observe, learn, admire, and do what they do.*

Live faithfully.

» Raise the roof for the prodigal.

» Pray regularly for your pastor and his or her family.

» Love . . . even though . . .

» Trust God. Until it hurts.

» Embark on a spiritual pilgrimage.

» Watch *The Passion of the Christ*.

» Get baptized.

» Build up, don't tear down, the body of Christ.

» Teach another person how to study the Bible in depth.

» Read Psalm 119 in its entirety. Read it again.

» Fast and pray for the nation of Israel.

» Visit a monastery for a weekend. Or an entire week.

» Pray with expectation.

Do something radical.

▶ Go on a spiritual pilgrimage.

▶ Become a missionary.

▶ Join the Peace Corps.

▶ Simplify your lifestyle, and sell your possessions.

▶ Make a 180-degree change in your career.

▶ Live in a motor home.

- Join a rock-and-roll band.

- Take a job in another country.

- Become a street musician.

- Go to seminary.

- Adopt a child.

Be a better parent.

▶ Point out to your kids—no matter their age—what they are doing right.

▶ Show them affection. Don't worry—you can't overdo it.

▶ Make eye contact when you speak to your kids.

▶ Support their passions.

▶ Tell them you love them (even if you never had parents say that to you).

- Tell them, "I believe in you."
  Then show them.

- Encourage them. (Keep it real.
  They can smell insincerity.)

- Listen to your kids.
  Stop interrupting.

- Give them grace.

- Do these things even if you don't
  feel comfortable.

Adopt SMART goals.

S: A goal must be *specific*. For example, "I want to get a new job" is wishful thinking. That sentiment becomes a goal when you commit to: "I will send out ten resumes every day for the next month."

M: A goal must be *measurable*. If you can't measure it, you probably can't accomplish it. Measurement is a way of monitoring your progress.

A: A goal must be *achievable*: it should be out of reach enough to be challenging, but it should not be out of sight. Otherwise it becomes discouraging.

R: A goal must be *realistic*. If you want to lose fifty pounds in thirty days, you are not being realistic.

T: A goal must be *time-bound*. There should be a start date and an end date.

Live a life of love and laughter.

» Determine that everywhere you go, you will make babies giggle.

» Walk through Disneyland after hours.

» Throw a big pool party. Ask everyone to bring a different animal floatie.

» Grow your own ginormous vegetable and enter it in the county fair.

» Get a pen pal. And write to him or her with an actual pen and paper!

» Talk like a pirate for a day.

» Take a tap-dancing lesson.

» Call into a radio talk show, and give your opinion. Behave.

» Attend a Harvest Crusade.

» Watch (and pretend you enjoy) movies with subtitles.

» Eat a Dodger Dog at Dodger Stadium.

» Attend a U2 concert.

» Embrace the humor of Patsy Clairmont.

» Don't underestimate the power of Play-Doh.

» Trace your family roots.

Get centered.

Psalm 118:8 stands at the exact center of the Bible and proclaims this truth: "It is better to take refuge in the LORD than to trust in man." The very center axis of the Bible is a great reminder to trust in God over ourselves or other people.

Ask yourself: *Is God's Word at the center of my life? Is there any thing or any person in my life that has edged God out?* Write those things down, and ask God to help you get back on track and restore balance.

Celebrate the ache.

When you start exercising, it's okay to ache. Be assured, that first day of walking, rowing, or hiking will not kill you. I promise. But yes, you're gonna be hurting the next day.

But as you ache, thank God for the meticulous way He created you: for the way organs, muscles, cartilage, and bones work in synchronicity to get you up that hill or even through an average workday. As you sweat, praise God's holy genius in creation and affirm His love for you. And when you hit that last ten minutes on the elliptical, remember what Nike says: *no one has ever regretted it.*

REAL-LIFE CHALLENGE: *Start doing twenty minutes of exercise every other day this week. Increase that as you feel comfortable.*

Start a blog.

Writing a blog will challenge you as well as connect you to others in a whole new way. Blogging
can be a creative, social, evangelistic, and even
profitable endeavor. You'll be amazed at the
friendships and influence you can gain by simply sharing your expertise and finding common
ground with people located five miles or five
thousand miles away. Oh yeah, another benefit
of blogging: it makes you look cool!

REAL-LIFE CHALLENGE: *This week visit
some blogs you admire. Study why those blogs
work well and what elements inspire you. Leave
a comment. Begin using blogs to connect with
people.*

Don't let age be an excuse.

Don't be fooled. Many people—of all ages—are walking around alive, but that in no way means they are truly *living*. Do you, for instance, live as if your best years are behind you? What dreams have you written off? What are you sitting around *not* doing? If you have stopped your own clock or moved up your expiration date, you are living contrary to God's good plans for you—and frankly, you stand in direct opposition to His authority *over you*.

If you woke up today with your heart beating and your lungs pumping, remember that God has a purpose for this day as well as for your life. He is the Author and Finisher of everything that is you. To live on less than that miracle is to go nose-to-nose with the Creator of the universe (not a good plan). It may be time to recharge the engines and do some serious CPR on your life, your perspective, and your dreams!

Never allow age be your excuse for not doing anything. Consider what these silver successes accomplished in the second half of people's lives:

- Benjamin Franklin played an instrumental role in drafting and signing the Declaration of Independence. He was seventy.

- Leonardo da Vinci drew sketches even in his sixties.

- Leo Tolstoy was writing novels into his seventies.

- Michelangelo sculpted until he was eighty-nine.

- Mother Teresa ministered to the poor and dying until she was eighty-seven.

- Famed American folk artist Grandma Moses began painting in her seventies after abandoning embroidery because of arthritis.

- Colonel Sanders was sixty-five when his chicken finally caught on.

- Laura Ingalls Wilder published her first *Little House* book at sixty-five.

- Julia Child published *Mastering the Art of French Cooking* at fifty.

- Japanese businessman Momofuku Ando invented instant ramen noodles. He was forty-eight.

REAL-LIFE CHALLENGE: *Find the most active peers you know, and hang out with them. Ask them their secrets to staying young physically and mentally.*

Live your dreams.

» Shop at your local farmers market.

» Take a sabbatical.

» Become an amateur chef.

» Hang out in a café in Taos,
New Mexico, and write.

» Audition for a local theater company.

» Experience New York at
Christmastime.

» Write and submit an article about something you're passionate about.

» Volunteer on a political campaign.

» Ice skate in Central Park.

» Meet your favorite author.

» Stay in a villa in Tuscany, Italy.

» Walk on fire.

» Make things better. Start a petition.

Nosh on the exotic.

- Grasshoppers in Thailand

- Escargot (snails) in France

- Fried spider in Cambodia

- Fugu (blowfish) in Japan

- Iguana in El Salvador

- Silkworm larvae in Korea

- Cow lips in Madagascar

- Tuna eyes in Japan

- Chitlins (pig intestines) in the Deep South

- Jellied moose nose (yes, as in Bullwinkle) in the northernmost US

- Rocky mountain oysters (also known as prairie oysters or cowboy caviar) in the western US

- Armadillo eggs (cheese stuffed jalapeños) in Texas

- Monkey toes in Indonesia

- Seal flipper pie in Canada

Don't be a slave to emotions.

One key to growing faith and putting on the new self God has given you is to recognize when emotions begin to boss you around. You can stare at a Bible verse for an hour, memorize it, and speak it passionately to another person—but that does not mean it owns any solid ground in your life, that it has taken root and actually changed you.

Emotions are very real. They are loud, beautiful, and brilliant expressions of God's divine workmanship. But emotions do not carry power and authority over you. Identify yourself with the Word; allow His Word and His truth to carry greater weight than your emotions. Tame your emotions with truth:

- *Guilt*: Psalm 32:5

- *Insecurity*: Joshua 1:9

- *Worry*: Philippians 4:6–9

- *Regret*: Philippians 3:13–14

Take a road trip
through US history.

» Washington, DC

» Colonial Williamsburg, Virginia

» Philadelphia, Pennsylvania

» Boston, Massachusetts

» Charleston, South Carolina

» Richmond, Virginia

» Franklin, Tennessee

Explore the tropics of Panama.

It's easy to fall in love with Panama. Located at the waist of the Americas, Panama is just a few degrees north of the equator. Its location—thanks to the engineering marvel of the Panama Canal—is a vital economic passage that offers access to several countries, all within a few hours of each other.

For a few short years, our family lived in Panama and experienced its culture and beauty up close. Our high-rise in Panama City over-looked the famed canal. Watching the ships pass through the locks of the canal at dusk and hearing the creaks and moans of steel pierce the evening stillness is forever etched in my mind. But there's so much more to this amazing country than just the canal.

Specifically, there are the people—some of the warmest, most welcoming in the world. Panama City is a financial center that has attracted a beautiful, thriving mix of nationalities. Beyond the city limits, the country is home to seven Indian groups, as well as Afro-Caribbeans and West African descendants, which makes traveling between the big city and remote villages a cultural excursion. Panama has the same outdoor activities and incredible landscapes as its more popular neighbor Costa Rica—but with far fewer tourists. The more than 950 species of birds in Panama attract people from around the world, and the locals will tell you exactly how to get to the more remote white-water rivers, small islands, and powdery beaches.

Must-sees:

- the towering churches and grand plazas of Casco Viejo

- the ruins of Panamá Viejo

- the magnificent islands of The Archipiélago de las Perlas

- Isla Tobaga's beaches and colorful villages

- the rainforest of Parque Natural Metropolitano

- the world's most amazing shortcut—the Panama Canal

Live with compassion.

» Be nice to cats. They can't help it.

» Treat the act of saying grace with fresh reverence.

» Make an anonymous donation to a worthy cause.

» Help the next generation.

» Don't flip past commercials about needy children. Give. Generously.

» Befriend the office grouch.

» Work at a soup kitchen at Thanksgiving. Go back the following Tuesday and serve again.

» Whenever possible, recognize and reward teachers.

» Help build a well in a developing country.

» Go to a senior center and hand out flowers. Pray with those who want to pray.

» One day a week, make yourself completely available to others.

» Visit a sick friend in the hospital.

» Give your neighbor a day off. Volunteer to take his or her kids to the zoo (no, you can't leave them in the monkey habitat).

Tell them.

It could be the guy next to you at the office, whom you've shared jokes with for years. It could be the woman next to you on the bus or the teenager who mows your lawn. It could be an old friend from high school who has reached out to you online, or it could very well be a person in your Bible study.

You see, everyone needs Jesus.

To help us recognize that fact, our perfect God left a missing piece in each one of us. That void will forever draw men and women to His heart. Will you tell them about Jesus? Will you simply share your "before" and "after" story? Think about it.

There is a God-shaped vacuum in the heart of every man which cannot be filled by any created thing, but only by God, the Creator, made known through Jesus.
—Blaise Pascal

REAL-LIFE CHALLENGE: *Tune your heart to the hearts of those around you. Think about those you know who need to meet Jesus Christ. Trust God to lead that next conversation.*

Ask yourself the tough questions.

- What are my life priorities? In what ways are they obvious in the way I live?

- Where does God fit into my daily routine?

- Is God honored by how I spend my time? my money?

- What specific actions have I taken lately to advance my goals?

- What negative habits need to go?

- In what areas of my life is God's hand currently moving?

- In what ways have I been giving to others?

- How is my prayer life?

Bring back the word *repent*.

I'm a genuine, Holy Ghost, Jesus-filled, preachin' machine this mornin'!

—Sonny, in *The Apostle*

Unless you hang out in big tent revivals, you might be uncomfortable—at least a little—with the call to "repent!" For me it conjures up images of scandal-ridden televangelists or the Robert Duvall movie *The Apostle*.

Still, outside of the word *love*, *repentance* may be the most powerful, life-giving word in a Christian's experience. The cross symbolizes repentance, the church was established to welcome repentance, and regardless of our denomination or the baggage we bring individually, each of us must embrace repentance when we vow to follow Christ.

If we as God's people want to make a meaningful impact on this world, we need to seriously—and consistently—repent before God. The Bible is clear about the importance of repentance. Second Chronicles 7:14 says, "If my people, who are called by my name, will humble themselves and pray and seek my face and turn from their wicked ways, then will I hear from heaven and will forgive their sin and heal their land."

REAL-LIFE CHALLENGE: *Study repentance. Read Luke 24:47; Ezekiel 18:30–32; 2 Peter 3:9; Matthew 4:17. Meditate on what God shows you. Try repentance firsthand. Discover the freedom God unleashes in your life when you truly repent before Him. Step into this week with a light heart and a clean slate!*

Live a life of love and laughter.

» In honor of Ferris Bueller, take the day off.

» Be bold. Wear bling. Land somewhere between Dr. Dre and Princess Di.

» Own a bottle of expensive cologne or perfume. Wear it!

» Read the *Little House on the Prairie* series to your kids or grandkids.

» Chase down the ice cream truck. Buy one of everything.

» Play in the rain with your kids or grandkids.

» Eat a hot dog in Central Park.

» Go see back-to-back comedies at the cinema. Laugh and eat chocolate until you pop.

» See the leaves change in Tennessee.

» Visit Graceland in Memphis. As you walk around, try for just one percent of Elvis's swagger.

» Spoil babies.

» Be it a canoe, a rowboat, a speedboat, or a yacht, own your own boat.

Think "big picture."

The great evangelist Leonard Ravenhill was the last person on the planet you'd ever accuse of mincing words. "Five minutes after you die, you'll know how you should have lived."

You've got 1,440 minutes today; 43,200 this month; and 525,600 this year to determine your priorities and how you should be living. Even those minutes aren't guaranteed. So how *will* you live?

As distracted as we sometimes get, we can't afford to lose sight of the bigger picture—that heaven, our true home, awaits. Today carries real pain, struggle, and obligations, but never cast aside your "light and momentary troubles" for the eternal glory that outweighs them all (2 Corinthians 4:17)! Your citizenship in heaven begins on earth. Live a life that has heaven's flavor all over it.

REAL-LIFE CHALLENGE: *Elizabeth Barrett Browning said, "Earth's crammed with heaven . . . but only he who sees takes off his shoes." As a sweet, simple reminder this week, take off your shoes whenever God gives you a glimpse of heaven. It will be a thank-You nod from you to Him.*

Find the mute button on life.

Studies show that, on average, each person sees two thousand media images per day, that women speak an average of twenty thousand words a day, and that men use seven thousand words. That's a lot of noise!

No one is quick to share that life *really does* have a mute button. It's there! We just refuse to hit it.

REAL-LIFE CHALLENGE: *Silence life. Home in on God's voice for the first thirty minutes of your day. Allow God to own your thoughts before you flip on the television, cell phone, or computer or before you fire up your conversation button.*

Stop comparing yourself to others.

 Be who God meant you to be and you will set the world on fire.
—Catherine of Siena

If you could tally up the actual hours you've spent comparing yourself to other people, you might be shocked to find that you've handed over hours, days, maybe even years of your life. This comparing might be subtle, or it could clearly be influencing your daily decisions and actions. Either way, such comparing is a sure way to forfeit the life God has uniquely designed you to live. If this is a problem for you, here are some steps you can take:

- **Confess to God**. Confess your heart issue, and ask Him to reveal the root of those thoughts. If there's ego or pride, surrender that.

- **Affirm truth**. Every day, read scriptures (truth) to affirm your worth to God and His love for you.

- **Limit media**. Many times, advertising, television, and social media form a crowd of pressure around us that feeds our insecurities, and we don't even realize it.

- **Renew your mind daily**. This isn't a one-time thing. Putting on the new man or woman we are in Christ is a daily discipline (Colossians 3:10)

- **Remember**. Remember who you are, what you've accomplished, and that nothing can destroy what God is doing in your life right now.

REAL-LIFE CHALLENGE: *Read Psalm 139. Focus on the love and care in crafting you!*

Go tech: connect!

Sometimes, separation caused by distance or even lifestyle differences makes it far too easy to lose touch with those we've been called to love and shepherd. Let technology help you bridge that gap between you and your kids or grandkids. Learning a few online tools is easy— and, like it or not, it's how they communicate.

- Read a book to your kids or grandkids via Skype.

- Have breakfast together via video chat or a Google+ hangout.

- Text them once a week to tell them you are thinking of them.

- Friend them on Facebook. Once in a while, post a note of encouragement. Don't overdo it, though, or you'll get the ax!

- Record a video message from time to time, and e-mail it to your kids or grandkids.

- Share humorous links, videos, and stories. Stay relevant about things they're interested in.

- Send them iTunes or iPhone app gift cards.

Live an adventure.

» Visit San Francisco's Fisherman's Wharf.

» Visit Easter Island.

» Climb Mount Fuji in Japan.

» Visit the Phi Phi islands in Thailand.

» Visit the Greek Island of Santorini. Be astonished.

» Ride the London Eye.

» Climb the steps of Mayan ruins.

» Visit the Galapagos Islands.

» Participate in the Tour de France.
Okay, just cheer on the pack.

» Camp in the Alaskan wilderness.
Bring ear muffs!

» Visit Stockholm, Sweden.

» Visit Pompeii.

» See the incredible tree root systems of
Angkor Wat in Cambodia.

» Visit Costa Rica.

Plant something to celebrate.

Ritual and tradition link one generation to the next and can often help us pass along our faith.

Mark occasions—both good and difficult—with your children or grandchildren by planting something (tree, bush, flowers) together. Watching a tree grow over time gives you an opportunity to talk about God's constant presence through the highs and lows of life. And it's a tradition that's easy to pass along!

REAL-LIFE CHALLENGE: *Get a small rosemary bush, and plant it with your child or grandchild. Watch it grow, snip its leaves once in a while, and together, use it in your evening meal.*

Admit that you blew it.

Confession—or admitting you blew it—shouldn't be a yearly event that the people around you need to purchase tickets for. Instead, admit your mistakes as part of everyday life. Make it as common as mowing your lawn or washing your car. Simply own the offense or misstep. Share honestly when you make a bad decision, let someone down, don't follow through, or don't do what you sense God telling you to do. Give people around you the opportunity to see God's redemptive power actively at work in you.

REAL-LIFE CHALLENGE: *Be quick to confess this week. Don't rationalize or dismiss mistakes. Be the first to admit, "Hey, that was my fault," or to say, "I apologize. I shouldn't have spoken in that tone. Will you forgive me?"*

Ask God first.

Asking God *first* is a no-brainer for Christians—or is it? Often we pick up the phone instead of taking our concerns to God's throne. We pace. We ponder. We try to work out by our own reasoning and with our own network of resources. We often, by habit, leapfrog over the first and true Source of power: Jesus Christ. The following saints of God asked Him for help, and we should too:

- Hannah prayed for a son (1 Samuel 1:11).

- Gideon prayed for a sign from God (Judges 6:36–39).

- Solomon prayed for wisdom (1 Kings 3:5–9).

- Daniel prayed for mercy (Daniel 9:16–19).

- Jonah prayed for deliverance (Jonah 2:2–9).

- Jesus prayed, asking God to "take this cup from me" (Luke 22:42).

- Paul prayed for spiritual strength for his flock (Ephesians 3:14–21).

REAL-LIFE CHALLENGE: *Study the prayers of believers who have gone before us. Be inspired by their prayers, and learn to go to God first and to trust Him in all things.*

Let God fight for you.

The day was officially spiraling. The Israelites had Pharaoh's army and the fury of hell at their heels as they fled Egypt. But they kept walking forward in spite of the life-threatening circumstances around them. They ultimately believed that God would rescue them—and He did.

Had God's people been led by emotion and circumstance, they would have been led by fear. The human desire to be right, to be heard, or to go down in a blaze of glory is not what spared the Israelites that day. Faith in God and trust in His power and His promises saved them.

Living a life that's bigger than you requires standing down and letting God be the hero even though—and especially when—the odds are mounting against you.

The Lord will fight for you, and you have only to be silent.
—Exodus 14:14 ESV

Live faithfully.

» Read Brother Lawrence's *The Practice of the Presence of God*. Aspire to maintain an unbroken conversation with God.

» Learn to pray the scriptures.

» Explore what it means to be a servant-leader.

» Draw closer to God. Study the spiritual disciplines of prayer, Bible study, worship, solitude, and fasting. Make these parts of your everyday life.

» Go to a big tent revival. Respond.

» Pray for and support national and world missions.

» Commit yourself to a ministry 100 percent.

» Take your faith to the next level.

» Write a love letter to God.

» Live as if heaven really is on earth.

» Float on the Dead Sea.

» Develop a heart like evangelist Billy Graham.

» Write like King David. Pray like Paul.

» Forgive someone. Completely.

» Live a life of contagious worship.

» Sit in an empty church and talk to God.

» Live a life of contagious worship.

» The next time God nudges you, answer Him, "Here I am, Lord. Send me."

Write your dad an IOU.

He juggled bills. He worked overtime. He pushed aside a dream or two. He lost sleep, waited up, and eventually cheered you on as he let you go. Hopefully, you have a dad that fits this description. I sure do.

Love motivated your dad to provide for you and care for you through the years. Of course, he wasn't perfect, but he did his best, just as you are doing in your life. Now it's your turn to give back—in both grace and gratitude.

REAL-LIFE CHALLENGE: *Write your dad an IOU for all his sacrifices. Let him know how grateful you are. Promise to pay him back by living well and carrying his love, faith, strength, and legacy into the future.*

Live in the light.

Nothing is more confusing than trying to find something in the dark. You'll trip, fumble, and maybe even lose a tooth before you can flip on the light. God's Word is just like that light— Scripture keeps us from fumbling, from being lost in the shadows, grasping, tripping, and wandering. The light helps us discern spiritual danger so we can avoid it, and it points our heart and eyes in the right direction. It points us to God.

REAL-LIFE CHALLENGE: *Light a candle, perhaps when you get home at night, to designate your sacred space, set apart from the confusing shadows of the world. Seek God in that quiet place. Let the light of His Word minister to your heart and make clear the path you are to take.*

Inject some spontaneity.

There's an app to synchronize your calendar to every other calendar on the planet and an app to remind you when to floss. Lose all the apps, your smartphones, and your compulsive scheduling—at least for a day. Okay, at least for an hour! Practice spontaneity. Have some fun already!

- Throw a spur-of-the-moment party.

- Go on an unplanned vacation.

- Bust out a dance move.

- Leave work early and go on a hike.

- Sing a cappella—whatever, wherever!

- Buy flowers for someone.

- Call an old friend.

- Go catch a movie by yourself.

REAL-LIFE CHALLENGE: *Don't get bogged down in the details and stay in your rut. Think of something crazy you could do today— and do it!*

Create a family cookbook.

The edges of our little family cookbook are tattered; every other page is splattered with oil or remnants of some bubbly concoction that leapt from its pot.

The cookbook's cover has been missing since 1998. Still, this family cookbook we made a few years after we got married is my go-to for some of our family's favorite recipes. There's Grandma Cox's corn casserole, Aunt Tony's nutty buddy treats, my mother-in-law Linda's wilted salad, Aunt Leezah's balsamic strawberry salad, and Mom's amazing merlot sauce.

Don't let those family recipes go! Record them, enjoy them, celebrate the people who shared them, and pass them down for generations.

REAL-LIFE CHALLENGE: *Along with each recipe, ask every relative to submit a piece of news that happened in his or her life. Bam! Your cookbook is now a news update! (Watch out. Aunt Diane may want a new one every year!)*

Kiss without guilt.

There are twenty-six calories in a Hershey's Kiss. Oddly enough, it's estimated that you can burn approximately twenty-six calories in a one-minute kiss. So eat kisses—and give kisses—abundantly.

Sail Antarctica.

To breathe in some of the world's most surreal beauty, take a sailing trip through Antarctica. You'll spot penguin colonies, iceberg-clogged coves, and frozen islands. Enjoy nearly twenty-four hours of daylight, and listen to the constant groan and splash of glaciers. You'll get to feel the southernmost part of the earth beneath your feet and explore dormant volcanoes.

Live an adventure.

» Go on a cross-country ski trek.

» Conquer at least one Polar Bear Club swim for charity.

» Visit Ireland on St. Patrick's Day.

» Ski the Alps.

» Visit the West Coast of Scotland.

» Pan for gold.

» Visit the 1200 islands of Maldives.

» Kayak the Colorado River.

» Visit Stonehenge in England.

» Sail around the world.

» Water-ski barefoot.

» Visit Los Glaciares National Park
in Argentina.

Try unconditional love.

Everyone longs to be loved. You'd think that since we're all after the same thing, we'd be better at loving the way the gospel tells us to love: Love is patient. Love is kind. Pretty simple, huh? But how are you doing at loving others? Is your love weighed down with conditions? With expectations? Have you added your own fine print to your love agreements? Try loving God's way—unconditionally. *Unconditionally* is defined as without limitation or conditions.

Go ahead. Try it. When it comes to loving God's way, you've got absolutely nothing to lose.

Avoid crowds.

When God sets you apart, rescues you from the brink of death, and sets you high in a place of honor, He also marks you with His holiness. You inherit divine traits you never could have wrangled on your own. His love and power transform you, and soon it becomes impossible—and unpalatable—to follow the crowd. Author Brennan Manning says this in his book *Abba's Child*: "Define yourself radically as one beloved by God. This is the true self. Every other identity is illusion."

Following the crowd means falling back into the old you and clips the wings with which God has fashioned you to soar. Putting shackles back on your feet makes no sense. While some people view the Christian life as a list of cans and can'ts, they've yet to taste the freedom of living in the presence of God.

REAL-LIFE CHALLENGE: *The next time you feel yourself following the crowd, remember this: you've been called out and set apart. Don't exchange God's extraordinary call for anything that resembles ordinary! Get in His presence and let go of your crowd mentality.*

Visit the locations of some of your favorite movies.

- *Field of Dreams*: Dyersville, Iowa

- *Star Wars*: Death Valley in California and Tunisia

- *Pirates of the Caribbean*: The Bahamas

- *Lord of the Rings*: Tongariro National Park in New Zealand

- *Shawshank Redemption*: Ohio State Reformatory in Mansfield, Ohio

- *Rocky* (the stairs): Philadelphia Museum of Art in Philadelphia, Pennsylvania

- *Grease*: Venice High School in Venice, California

- *Dead Poets Society*: St. Andrew's School in Middletown, Delaware

- *Sleepless in Seattle* (houseboat): Seattle's Lake Union harbor

- *From Here to Eternity*: Halona Cove on Oahu, Hawaii

- *Armageddon* and *Superman: The Movie*: Grand Central Station on 42nd Street in Manhattan, New York City

Give your opinion . . . less.

It's a humbling and abrupt awakening when we realize the world has not formed a line outside our front door anxiously awaiting the moment we emerge with our opinion on the matter. Think about it: When's the last time someone called you and said, "I *must* get your opinion on something!" or, "If you don't speak with me about this decision immediately, it will ruin my life!"?

Opportunities to speak into others' lives *will* come. Until then, resist the urge to splurge with words, and zip it.

> Do nothing out of selfish ambition or vain conceit, but in humility consider others better than yourselves.
>
> —Philippians 2:3

REAL-LIFE CHALLENGE: *The next time you attend a gathering, simply observe the conversation as it flows around you. Determine not to interrupt, interject, or throw in your two cents.*

Create a one-word epitaph.

If you could have only one word etched on your tombstone when you die, what would you want that word to be? The word doesn't have to describe who you are right now, but who you hope to become by the end of your life. Would it be *talented*, *passionate*, or *successful*? Or perhaps *disciple*, *faithful*, or *honest*? Choose a word that challenges you, honors God, and inspires your friends and family to live more intentionally.

Live your dreams.

» Cut down a Christmas tree on a snowy night.

» Get a makeover.

» Go clamming in Maine.

» See the Rose Bowl Parade in person.

» Build a business with heart.

» Inspire a crowd.

» Live in a foreign country.

» See *Madame Butterfly*.

» Rekindle the romance. Kiss your spouse like you mean it.

» Play golf at Pebble Beach.

» Learn to fence.

» Do one thing a month that scares you.

» Become bilingual.

Laugh at perfection.

Think about it. Perfection is totally uninspiring. It's overrated and also happens to be unattainable—but that's doesn't seem to deter some of us. We keep pursuing it!

Give up on perfection. In fact, laugh at the thought of it! Offer God and the world your beautifully broken and imperfect self. Snub flawlessness and christen today incredibly ordinary but packed with joy.

Understand the value of time.

It's likely one of the most common questions we ask ourselves: "Where does the time go?" Do you really want the answer to that question? If you knew, you might reevaluate how you slice up your time. Research suggests that, on average, we spend more than half of our lives on meaningless tasks. We spend:

- Five years standing in line

- Two years trying to return telephone calls

- Eight months opening direct mail

- Six years eating

- One year looking for misplaced objects

- Four years doing general household chores

- Twenty-five years sleeping

REAL-LIFE CHALLENGE: *This week, be conscious of how you spend your time. Make small changes along the way to reclaim your time. You could toss junk mail, declutter your home, prioritize your e-mail and phone habits, or get up an hour earlier.*

Get to know God.

To know *about* God and to truly determine to *know* God are two very different aspirations. When we understand the attributes of God—who He is in contrast to us—we begin to grasp how He will respond in good times and bad. When we live in a world where brick and mortar shelter us and where flesh and bone hold us upright, we forget the supernatural, not-of-this-world Spirit of God that guides, loves, and protects us. We do forget. Every day.

But when we study what He is like and *experience* a relationship with Him, the conclusion is unavoidable: God is nothing like us. He wouldn't run the world, the country, or a household the way we do. He does love us enough, however, to allow us to come to that conclusion on our own. Just as He loves us enough to wait until each of us turns around to love Him back . . . because He is Love.

Consider some of His attributes:

- **Omniscience**. He knows everything (Job 37:16).

- **Omnipotence**. He is all-powerful and brings to pass everything He chooses (Job 42:2).

- **Omnipresence**. He is present in all places at all times (Psalm 139:7).

- **Immutability**. God never changes (Hebrews 13:8).

- **Holiness**. God is utterly without sin (Psalm 99:9; Habakkuk 1:13).

- **Righteousness**. Righteousness is God's holiness revealed as He deals with us (Psalm 116:5; Ezra 9:15).

- **Sovereignty**. God rules His creation, knows what is best, and is in complete control of the universe and of history (Genesis 1:1; Revelation 1:17–18).

- **Love**. God doesn't just love us as an emotional expression. God *is* love. And His love encompasses His mercy, grace, and loving-kindness (1 John 4:7–21).

Live with compassion.

» Teach someone something.

» Put your parents and siblings on speed dial. Call often.

» Volunteer at a zoo.

» Teach someone to read.

» Share your business expertise with a new business owner.

» Learn the Heimlich maneuver.

» Serve in a women's shelter.

» Encourage a teenager every chance you get.

» Help organize a benefit concert.

» Fast for forty-eight hours. Give the money you saved to charity.

» Tip well.

» Look people in the eyes when they talk to you. Really listen.

» Always buy cookies from Girl Scouts. Even if you're on a diet.

» Become a foster parent.

Replace old messages.

▶ Replace "Try harder" with
"Trust God to make your way
straight and bless your efforts"
(see Proverbs 3:5–6).

▶ Replace "Look out for number
one" with "Honor others above
yourself" (see Mark 9:35).

▶ Replace "Fix the problem now"
with "Be joyful in hope, patient
in affliction, faithful in prayer"
(Romans 12:12).

▶ Replace "I need to get even"
with "Leave vengeance to God"
(see Romans 12:19).

- Replace "Strive for success" with "Love God with all your heart, mind, and soul" (see Matthew 22:37).

- Replace "I can never change" with "I can do all things through Christ who strengthens me" (Philippians 4:13 NKJV).

- Replace "I am a failure" with "I am fearfully and wonderfully made by God and created in His image" (see Psalm 139:13–14; Genesis 1:27).

- Replace "No one cares" with "I am the apple of God's eye, His beloved, created for purposes beyond understanding" (see Psalm 17:8; Jeremiah 29:11).

Break the rules once in a while.

Mark Twain was onto something when he said this:

> Life is short. Break the rules. Forgive quickly. Kiss slowly. Love truly. Laugh uncontrollably. And never regret anything that makes you smile.

Here are a few ways to get started breaking some rules this week:

- Eat dessert first.

- Skip work and go snowboarding.

- Play in fountains until you get caught.

- Attempt to barter at the mall.

- Buy a Slip 'n Slide—for yourself.

- Order off the kids' menu.

- Check out of your hotel room late.

- Mismatch your socks.

- Color outside the lines.

- Sing out loud whether or not you know the lyrics.

- Opt for pigtails.

- Run through the neighbors' sprinklers.

- Have a mouthful of snowflakes for lunch.

- Run in the hallway.

- Test-drive a Ferrari.

Live a life of love and laughter.

» What experiences have been amazing in your life? Do more of them!

» Organize a huge water balloon fight.

» Travel solo.

» Ride a cable car in San Francisco (while eating Rice-A-Roni).

» Learn how to make balloon animals.

» Ride a Segway through a beautiful city.

» Go to the Coca-Cola factory in Atlanta, Georgia.

» Try all thirty-three flavors of cheesecake at The Cheesecake Factory.

» Go on more hayrides.

» Ride that merry-go round—at any age!

» Go Christmas caroling with friends.

» Magnify the memories. Instead of one big vacation, budget for three small ones.

Watch the big ten on the big screen.

Watch the ten greatest movies of all time as ranked by the American Film Institute. If you want to see them on the big screen, find a historic or retro theater and request they put these in their lineup.

1. *Citizen Kane*
2. *Casablanca*
3. *The Godfather*
4. *Gone with the Wind*
5. *Lawrence of Arabia*
6. *The Wizard of Oz*
7. *The Graduate*
8. *On the Waterfront*
9. *Schindler's List*
10. *Singin' in the Rain*

Make amends.

So often we aren't living out our dreams—or even enjoying the day in front of us—because layers of bitterness, regret, or fear have caked around our hearts. Of course, that hardening is never part of the plan, but it happens. Whether we realize it or not—whether we admit it or not—those layers slowly extinguish possibility, joy, and hope. They also stunt our ability to love and receive love.

Today is the day you can change that, but it may take some courage and some humility. Pick up the phone. Write that letter. Send that e-mail. Remember, it's more important to be loving than to be right. Don't forfeit another day of joy to the things left undone.

Use heart metrics.

Author and leadership expert John Maxwell said that when God measures a man, He puts the tape around his heart, not his head. Try to do the same. Rather than look at the title, the size of the bank account, the number of degrees, or the size of a person's house, look at that person's actions.

Actions of the heart speak louder than words— every time.

Go on a news fast.

A study published in the *American Journal of Preventive Medicine* has found that too much negative TV can make you depressed and anxious. No doubt, a steady diet of murder, tragedy, and death can leave a person feeling insecure and unprotected. The solution? Give your brain a rest—at least for a little while. Turn off the bad news and regain your perspective. Yes, this fallen world is rife with chaos, but God is on the throne, and He really does have the whole world under His control. Hold fast to the truth of this timeless hymn:

> *Turn your eyes upon Jesus,*
> *Look full in His wonderful face,*
> *And the things of earth will grow*
> *strangely dim,*
> *In the light of His glory and grace.*
> —Helen H. Lemmel (1922)

Choose peace.

It's been said that when we are depressed, we are thinking about the past; when we are anxious, we are thinking about the future; but when live in the present, we can actually have peace.

Living in the present takes discipline and strength. To tame our thoughts and bring them under the loving, strong hand of God is not for the faint of heart. It's tough work! Here are five steps to get you going:

1. **Pray.** Prayer is a discipline that opens the door for peace (Philippians 4:6–7).
2. **Present.** Choose the present, not the past or the future (Matthew 6:34).
3. **Thank.** Inventory what you are grateful for in life (1 Thessalonians 5:18).
4. **Think.** Think about life-giving stuff (Philippians 4:8).
5. **Breathe.** Deeply. Repeat (Psalm 4:8).

Work hard, and grow your "grit."

Sometimes it seems as if our dreams will never materialize, as if everyone is passing us by and some of life's safes just can't be cracked. That's simply not true. Hard work and "grit"—that stubborn refusal to quit—are often the secrect combo that determines success. Here are a few people who didn't quit:

- Basketball greats Michael Jordan and Bob Cousy were each cut from their high school basketball teams.

- Beethoven's music teacher called him "hopeless" as a composer.

- It took director James Cameron fifteen years to make the movie *Avatar*.

- It took architect John Roebling ten years to overcome critics and get the Brooklyn Bridge approved and built.

- Director Steven Spielberg was rejected from the University of Southern California School of Theater, Film, and Television three times.

- Former vice president Dick Cheney flunked out of Yale University twice.

- Charles Schultz had every cartoon he submitted rejected by his high school yearbook staff.

- In 1954, the manager of the Grand Ole Opry fired Elvis Presley after one performance and told him, "You ain't goin' nowhere, son. You ought to go back to drivin' a truck."

- Henry Ford failed and went broke five times before he succeeded.

- A newspaper editor fired Walt Disney because he "lacked imagination and had no good ideas." Disney also went bankrupt several times before he built Disneyland.

- R. H. Macy failed seven times before his "little" store in New York City caught on.

- Twenty-one publishers rejected Richard Hooker's humorous war novel M*A*S*H. He had worked on it for seven years.

- It took writer Matthew Weiner seven years to pitch and get the TV hit *Mad Men* on the air.

- It took Noah one hundred years—and dismissing every critic in town—to build the ark.

Live an adventure.

» Visit the peaks of Machu Picchu, Peru.

» Visit Antelope Canyon near Page, Arizona.

» Walk in the crystal clear waters of Bora Bora Lagoon.

» Go see The Wave, a sandstone rock formation located near the Arizona/ Utah border.

» Take in the architectural grandeur of the Great Wall of China.

» Go swimming with stingrays (the tame ones) in the Cayman Islands.

» Go snorkeling at a shipwreck site.

» Bungee jump. Can't muster the courage? Then just jump extra high on your bed!

» Visit the Van Gogh Museum in Amsterdam.

» Stay overnight at the White House—legally. (It's a real program. The Lincoln Bedroom could be yours!)

» Visit Petra, Jordan, the city carved into rock.

» Hike the Grand Canyon.

Go on a safari.

▶ South Africa and Zambia: see lions, African elephants, leopards, black rhinoceroses, and Cape buffalo.

▶ India: see the largest population of Bengal tigers in the world.

▶ China: see the largest captive giant panda institution.

- Ecuador: see giant tortoises, fur seals, finches, and short-eared owls.

- Norway: see walruses, bearded seals, arctic fox, reindeer, and polar bears.

- Thailand: take an excursion into the Thai jungle, and learn to ride an elephant.

Read the good stuff.

I'm talking about the classics.

- *Confessions* by Saint Augustine

- *Mere Christianity* by C. S. Lewis

- *The Knowledge of the Holy* by A. W. Tozer

- *The Pilgrim's Progress* by John Bunyan

- *Foxe's Book of Martyrs* by John Foxe

- *The Imitation of Christ* by Thomas à Kempis

- *The Practice of the Presence of God* by Brother Lawrence

- *The Cost of Discipleship* by Dietrich Bonhoeffer

- *My Utmost for His Highest* by Oswald Chambers

- *The Christian's Secret of a Happy Life* by Hannah Whitall Smith

Read the good stuff.

And here are more recent titles:

- *Grace for the Moment* by Max Lucado

- *Experiencing God* by Henry Blackaby

- *Celebration of Discipline* by Richard Foster

- *What's So Amazing About Grace?* by Philip Yancey

- *Jesus Calling* by Sarah Young

- *Redeeming Love* by Francine Rivers

- *Following Jesus* by N. T. Wright

- *Crazy Love* by Francis Chan

- *Heaven* by Randy Alcorn

Live with strength.

» Learn how to receive a compliment gracefully.

» Take a walk on the beach at night. Move in step with the moonlight.

» Do what you were created to do— and figure out how to make a living doing it.

» Create an honest piece of writing.

» Learn how to take criticism.

» Learn to let go.

» Make love a habit.

» Forgo gossip. For good.

» Choose to do meaningful work.

» Celebrate small and big wins in your life.

» Live with intention—in your relationships, your work, and your faith.

Create a morning ritual.

It's not a commandment from God, but waking up early sure isn't a bad idea. If you want to boost your productivity and get a jump on your day, try establishing a morning ritual. Watch the sun rise. Meet with God; converse with Him; commit to Him that—with His help—you will not waste the gift of this day. Don't forget to toast the potential of the day with some piping hot coffee (also a gift!).

> Rising very early in the morning, while it was still dark, [Jesus] departed and went out to a desolate place, and there he prayed.
>
> —Mark 1:35 ESV

Give honest answers.

The next time you ask someone, "How are you?" and the response is, "Great!" just remember that this may be a cover for a person who is really hurting. Gauge whether you can gently encourage the other person to tell you how he or she *really* is.

The same goes for *your* responses. Ditch the mask. Be honest. Live authentically. You might be surprised to see that the quality of your relationships grows as your honesty increases. (And by the way, you aren't fooling anyone. No one is "Great!" all the time.)

Hike the Inca Trail.

The Inca Trail combines culture, nature, and history thanks to its rich past. Trek mountain and subtropical jungles, and see the tunnels and ruins of Peru. This incredible hike can be taken in four days.

Ride horseback through Mongolia.

Close your eyes and imagine it: you're galloping under sapphire skies as a Mongolian wind tugs at your hair and a strapping horse carries you across a rugged terrain. Channel your inner Indiana Jones (or Genghis Khan), and strike out on a Mongolian adventure!

Learn to want what you already have.

It's been said that gratitude turns what we have into enough. That reminder injected into everyday life might very well remedy the plague of depression and anxiety. Still, we continue to strive for more. Why? Because we've learned to strive, and what's learned becomes easy. Striving is what we're programmed to do.

The harder thing—and the thing that is needed—is to recognize when our desire for power or possession overshadows worthy, God-breathed goals. It may sound easy, but it takes constant focus, prayer, and discernment to keep your heart in check. Remember, the enemy has come to kill, steal, and destroy, and he does that in subtle, stealthy, and underhanded ways. You won't see a neon sign that says "misplaced desire" or "wrong-way street."

REAL-LIFE GOAL: *Rather than constantly striving for things you don't have, try being thankful for what you already possess. The list of blessings you identify may amaze you!*

Visit these ten places in the US.

A lifetime isn't long enough to discover and appreciate the history, nostalgia, and eclectic cultures of the United States. Here are just a few places to be sure to visit if you ever get the chance. Yes, there are a zillion more, but let's pace ourselves, shall we?

1. New Orleans, Louisiana: for its spirit, people, culture, music and cuisine.

2. Austin, Texas: for its green spaces, live music, funky boutiques, and cozy coffee shops.

3. Times Square, New York: for its energy, diversity, mega-signage, fashion, and architecture.

4. Los Angeles, California: for its fun array of beaches, entertainment, pop culture, restaurants, and creative inhabitants.

5. Nashville, Tennessee: for its country music, southern hospitality, down-home food, and artistic community.

6. Boulder, Colorado: for its outdoor adventures, coffee shops, and "healthy" and inspired ambiance.

7. Santa Fe, New Mexico: for its stunning Spanish Pueblo Revival architecture and overall creative vibe.

8. Maui, Hawaii: for its exotic beaches, resorts, stunning sunsets, friendly natives, and otherworldly terrains.

9. US Virgin Islands and Puerto Rico: for their amazing beaches and landscapes (yes, they are US territories and only a flight away).

10. Charleston, South Carolina: for its historic antebellum architecture and southern flair.

Live a life of love and laughter.

» Walk with your sweetheart on the beach. Talk about your dreams.

» Learn everything your smartphone can do.

» Learn the constellations. Stargaze with the one you love.

» Catch fireflies with the neighborhood kids.

» Eat a cheesesteak in Philly.

» Take a cake-decorating class.

» Become a barista.

» Learn how to make handmade paper.

» Record an album of you singing.
  (It's easier than you think.)

» Run through a field of wildflowers.

» Quit making bunny ears in photos.
  It's annoying.

» Get a photo of you "holding up" the
  Leaning Tower of Pisa.

» Experience a lantern festival.

» See a show at the Grand Ole
  Opry.

Attitude before altitude.

Most failure is determined in the beginning stages of trying anything new. Think about it: the gym, your running program, the new job, and that home improvement project. Most of our beginnings are subtly infected with the wrong attitude.

So get honest about your attitude. Is there value in what you are doing? Do you believe in yourself? Have you invited God to help you? What would happen if you quit? Make adjustments to your attitude where necessary—and then soar!

Live a life that sings.

Oliver Wendell Holmes observed that the average person goes to his grave with his music still in him. Maybe that silent song in you is clamoring to get out. Perhaps you have a heart for adoption or a whole new career in mind. Perhaps you dream of performing, fixing your marriage, or mustering up the courage to found a nonprofit.

What's the song that your heart quietly hums? What's the passion that's filling your spirit? What's keeping you quiet?

REAL-LIFE CHALLENGE: *Write down five things you need to do today to take that song from inside your heart and out into the world.*

Grab a hammer.

Find out where people in your community are building a Habitat for Humanity house, helping a family in need, or doing recovery work after a natural disaster. The sense of community you find as you serve will open new places of giving—and gratitude—in you.

- Visit habitat.org, and find out your options for donating time, money, or other resources to projects in your area.

- Contact your church and find out if there are areas where you can serve by lifting a hand, shovel, or hammer—raking leaves for the elderly, delivering meals, and more.

- Find out how you can lend a hand at organizations in your area such as food banks and shelters.

Get better, not bitter

Crisis. Betrayal. Injustice. Loss. Violence. Suffering. All are a part of daily life on a broken planet. In fact, it's enough to make a heart, well, bitter.

But that doesn't have to happen. Circumstances do not—and cannot—change the fact that God is sovereign, loving, and just. Bitterness—as described in Hebrews—is a root of deadly poison that makes it difficult to dig up and expose. Deep, stubborn, excruciating wounds sprout roots that only God's mighty hand can pull out, at which point He can then bring healing.

Healing is part of every equation. You just may not be there yet (and for some situations, healing may not be apparent this side of heaven). Choose today if you will let this trial claim your hope or reignite your faith, if you will become bitter, or if you will—by God's gracious work in your heart—get better.

> See to it that no one misses the grace of God and that no bitter root grows up to cause trouble and defile many.
>
> —Hebrews 12:15

Live an adventure.

» Backpack through Europe.

» Read *Blue Highways: A Journey into America* by William Least Heat-Moon. Grab a map, find the blue lines of the United States, and go!

» Hike the rain forest.

» Visit the wreckage of the Titanic in a submarine.

» Ride a motorcycle south on US Highway 1 in California.

» Learn to snowboard.

» Hop on that zip line and scream,
  "Wheeeee!"

» Walk the labyrinth at Chartres
  Cathedral near Paris, France.

» Go windsurfing.

» Become a professional treasure
  hunter.

» Visit Belgrade, Serbia.

» Watch a meteor shower. Take a sturdy
  umbrella.

Embrace grace.

Think about grace. Study it. Understand it as God's gift and very character. Be able to explain how essential God's grace is to your eternal future, as well as to your everyday life. Start here:

- We are saved by grace (Ephesians 2:8–9).

- We are "justified freely by God's grace" (Romans 3:24; see Titus 3:7).

- His grace is sufficient for us (2 Corinthians 12:9).

- We are "not under law, but under grace" (Romans 6:14–15).

- This age is the age of grace (Ephesians 3:2).

- We are to boldly approach the throne of grace in prayer (Hebrews 4:16).

Thirty people in thirty days.

Choose thirty people in your life, and on each of the next thirty days, tell one of those listed that you love him or her and why. Don't overthink the task. You can call, e-mail, post to a Facebook page, or send a handwritten note. Pray for the people you choose before you connect with them, and allow God to reveal Scripture, thoughts, or ways you might bless them. You'll be surprised by how expressing your thanks and love will strengthen your relationships and immediately enrich the quality of your life.

Be a hero.

A hero is a man who is afraid to run away.
—English proverb

Heroism is not always about rushing into a burning building. Look around. Heroic moments are happening everywhere. Whether it's helping an elderly person pump gas, checking up on a neighbor, or helping an overtaxed waitress remember her order, you can be someone's hero. Anytime. Anywhere.

To be others-focused means to be conscious of the conversation in your head and to flip the switch from "me" and "mine" to "us" and "ours." Think in terms of generosity, sacrifice, connection, noticing, and giving.

REAL-LIFE CHALLENGE: *Be others-focused. Look up from your routine. What is happening in the world around you? Notice things, notice people, and notice the direction the world is moving. Interact more with others. Pepper your path with heroic acts.*

Create a reverse bucket list.

If a bucket list stresses you out and shines a spotlight on everything you *haven't done* yet, then why not create a *reverse* bucket list? Write down your accomplishments in life to this point. When you're done, celebrate the spiritual, professional, and personal victories that have brought you to this day. Then break out the rocky road ice cream (apropos) for a sweet celebration of a road traveled with tenacity and grace. Here's my reverse bucket list:

- I was a starting point guard on my high school basketball team even though I was just a few hairs taller than a Shih Tzu.

- I refrained from killing my annoying brothers during our childhood, which likely thwarted a very lengthy prison stay (and eventually allowed us to become best friends).

- I've been to ten different countries and claim I can speak two languages (okay, British English is one of them).

- I fought and kicked an addiction.

- I survived being a news reporter, ethics intact.

- I am married to my true love.

- When my marriage broke, I worked hard to fix it rather than get a new one.

- I'm raising two kids who actually like me (for the moment anyway).

- I taught my children how to pray.

- I finished a half marathon.

- I've led a handful of people to Christ.

- I wrote that book.

- I conquered my fear of public speaking.

- I met two of my favorite authors—
  Alex Haley and Leo Buscaglia—
  before they died.

- I've become an entrepreneur who
  can ride any wave.

- I make a living at what God wired
  me to do.

- I often throw my hat up in the air
  on a crowded street like Mary Tyler
  Moore.

- I'd rather be with my family than
  anywhere else on the planet.

- I know which friends would move
  mountains for me if I asked.

- I've pursued God with great faith
  and with no faith—and found Him
  every time.

Go on a tour of strangely named cities.

- Fleatown, Ohio

- Bug Tussle, Oklahoma

- Yazoo City, Mississippi

- Possum Trot, Kentucky

- Rabbit Hash, Kentucky

- Santa Claus, Arizona

- Pumpkintown, Tennessee

- Nimrod, Minnesota

- Tarzan, Texas

- Tightwad, Missouri

- Spunky Puddle, Ohio

- Beans Purchase, New Hampshire

- Hoot and Holler Crossing, Texas

- Hot Coffee, Mississippi

- Half Hell, North Carolina

- Monkey Run, Missouri

- Frankenstein, Missouri

- Lizard Lick, North Carolina

- Burnt Water, Arizona

- Tick Bite, North Carolina

- Bucksnort, Alabama

- Boring, Oregon

- Goblin Town, Virginia

Live your dreams.

» Grow old with the one you love.

» Donate buckets of money to cancer research.

» Go see a Broadway play.

» Get a standing ovation.

» Make it onto the Kiss Cam at a ball game.

» Read books written by winners of the Nobel Prize in Literature.

» Build a company that includes profit sharing among employees, or institute it in your current workplace.

» Join Toastmasters International.

» Go on a safari. Dress like Jack Hanna.

» Run up the steps of the
   Philadelphia Museum of Art,
   and have your own Rocky
   moment.

» Live long enough to have Willard
   Scott show your face on a jelly jar.

» Watch the ball drop in Times Square
   on New Year's Eve.

» Be inspired: attend and cheer at a
   Paralympics or Special Olympics
   event.

Figure out "the one thing."

There's an unforgettable line in the movie *City Slickers* where the rugged cowboy Curly tells Mitch, the genteel city guy who is having a midlife crisis, that "The secret of life is . . . just one thing." It's then up to Mitch to figure out what his one thing is.

In the gospel of Luke, Jesus said something similar to Martha, after she complained about her sister, Mary, not serving the guests: "Only one thing is needed," He told her. When Jesus said that, everyone in the room got it. Mary—the one sitting at his feet and listening to Him all night—had figured out her "one thing."

And we need to figure it out for ourselves today. There are a million and one things we could pack into the next twenty-four hours. We have the same choice Mary did. Are we going to sit at Jesus' feet and listen, or will we throw ourselves into the vortex of today's demands?

REAL-LIFE CHALLENGE: *Spend fifteen minutes today reading from the Psalms. Tomorrow spend twenty minutes and the next day thirty minutes. Soon you'll be starting your day with thirty minutes to an hour doing the "one thing" that is needed.*

Obliterate fear.

The Bible contains enough "Fear nots" for nearly every day of the year. Fear is a funny thing. It's invisible. It has no tangible hands to hold us back or twist us into a knot, no strength to pin us down and threaten us. Yet it does. Every day. Fear keeps us from pursuing dreams, following ideas, or even fully living the day in front of us.

REAL-LIFE CHALLENGE: *Face just one of your fears today. Face another one tomorrow. Unravel it. Figure out its source. Pray about it. Allow God to overcome it—for good.*

Live a life of love and laughter.

» Ride a unicycle.

» Plan the perfect Valentine's Day. Spare no expense.

» Go to a drive-in movie.

» Visit a chocolate factory. Don't drink from the chocolate river!

» Learn how to beatbox.

» Throw a humongous surprise party.

» Swim with dolphins (not the football team).

» Learn to have a blast without blowing the bank.

» Join a band.

» Attend a concert at the Hollywood Bowl.

» Go on a tour of stars' homes in Hollywood.

» Scout out a jazz bar in the French Quarter of New Orleans.

» Be the life of the party.

» Offer to sign autographs even if you're not famous. (Don't knock it until you've tried it!)

Climb every mountain.

- Appalachian Trail, Georgia to Maine

- Pacific Crest Trail, California to Washington

- Grand Canyon National Park, Arizona

- Yosemite National Park, California

- Zion National Park, Utah

- Denali National Park Preserve, Alaska

- Mount Washington,
  New Hampshire

- Mount Rainier, Washington

- Longs Peak, Colorado

- Mount Shasta, California

- Mount Haleakala, Hawaii

- Mount Whitney, California

Make adventure an attitude.

You don't have to risk your life to have adventures; you simply have to be intentional about living fully each and every day. And that's all about *attitude*! Stepping into each day intent on living with an insatiable sense of wonder can change the contour of any twenty-four hours.

Everest expedition leader and motivational speaker John Amatt had it right when he said:

> Adventure isn't hanging on a rope off the side of a mountain. Adventure is an attitude that we must apply to the day-to-day obstacles of life—facing new challenges, seizing new opportunities, testing our resources against the unknown and, in the process, discovering our own unique potential.

Build something that will outlast you.

So often the day in front of us consumes us. Those days can become months, which become years. Think beyond this day and its pressures. If you are honest, you'll see that most everything around you—most everything you're working for—will eventually end up in a landfill somewhere.

Consider ways to give from your spirit, from that part of you crafted in heaven that thinks, sings, and creates. Maybe your legacy will be a piece of art, a statue, a memoir, or a house you design and build from scratch. You can write a song, a movie, or a book that will reach and influence the next generation. Teach, bless, and plant hope with the legacy you leave behind.

My Bucket List

....

....

....

....

....

....

....

My Bucket List

....

....

....

....

....

....

....

My Bucket List

....

....

....

....

....

....

....

My Bucket List

My Bucket List

....

....

....

....

....

....

....

My Bucket List

....

....

....

....

....

....

....

....

My Bucket List